LOVE
490

A Journey to Forgiveness

MARCIA M. WRIGHT

490 Love: A Journey to Forgiveness
Copyright © 2020 by Marcia M. Wright

All rights reserved. No part of this book may be reproduced or transmitted in any form or by any means, electronic or mechanical, including photocopying and recording, or by any information storage and retrieval system—with the exception of brief quotations in printed reviews—without prior permission in writing from the publisher at 490lovestudy@gmail.com.

All scripture quotations, unless otherwise indicated, are taken from the Holy Bible, New International Version®, NIV® Copyright© 1973, 1978, 1984, 2011, by Biblica, Inc.® Used by permission. All rights reserved worldwide.

Other Bible translations which are quoted in this book are listed on page 185, which by reference becomes part of this copyright page.

Names and identifying details in some stories have been changed to protect the identities of those involved.

Cover design by Kelly L. Howard
Page design services by ChristianEditingServices.com

For information about special quantity discounts of *490 Love: A Journey to Forgiveness* by churches and other special interest groups, please contact the publisher at 490lovestudy@gmail.com.

Trade paperback ISBN# 978-1-7352049-0-1

eBook ISBN# 978-1-7352049-0-1

To my parents, Bruce and Ruth Mosher,
thank you for always modeling Christ-like love and forgiveness to me.
This book wouldn't have happened without your example.

Table of Contents

Psalm 130   7
Acknowledgments   9
Introduction   11
What is Forgiveness?   15
F O R G I V E Acrostic   17

Chapter 1
    The Cross: Where Love and Forgiveness Intersect   19
    My Forgiveness Journey   23

Chapter 2
    He Forgave It All! Have You?   29
    My Daily Cross (with study questions)   37

Chapter 3
    Put Off the Old...Put on the New   47
    The Choice (with study questions)   57

Chapter 4
    Mercy Triumphs Over Judgment   67
    Halfway Down the Aisle (with study questions)   75

Chapter 5
    Who Do You Trust?   85
    If I Had Only Known... (with study questions)   91

Chapter 6
    Forgiveness Is a Key to Answered Prayer   105
    It Will Change Your Life (with study questions)   114

Chapter 7
    It's All About Love   125
    Loving the Unlovable (with study questions)   134

Chapter 8
    You Will Reap Exactly What You Sow—Only More of It   147
    Seeds of Bitterness (with study questions)   157

Appendix
    Forgiveness Acrostic Worksheet, and
        Memory Verse Checklist   170
    Should You Stay in an Abusive Relationship?   177
    Endnotes   183
    Bible Translations   185

Psalm 130

A song of ascents.

Out of the depths I cry to you, Lord;
Lord, hear my voice.
Let your ears be attentive to my cry for mercy.
If you, Lord, kept a record of sins,
Lord, who could stand?
But with you there is forgiveness,
so that we can, with reverence, serve you.
I wait for the Lord, my whole being waits,
and in his word I put my hope.
I wait for the Lord
more than watchmen wait for the morning,
more than watchmen wait for the morning.
Israel, put your hope in the Lord,
for with the Lord is unfailing love
and with him is full redemption.
He himself will redeem Israel
from all their sins.

Acknowledgements

There have been many people along the way who have helped make this book possible. First of all, I want to thank you, Jesus, for your gift of forgiveness on Calvary. You modeled the way of love and set the standard that you invite us to follow. My prayer is that your name will be glorified through this book and that people will be drawn to a closer walk with you.

John, I am so thankful that God chose you to be my husband. It has been a wild ride! We have learned so much from each other over the years. Thank you for your support while I have been writing this book. Your encouragement and belief in the message that I feel God has asked me to share helped make *490 Love: A Journey to Forgiveness* possible. This is your book too.

Anya, my joy, I thank God every day that he granted me the privilege of being your mother. You have always forgiven my shortcomings and loved me anyway. Thank you! I am so proud of the young lady that you are becoming, and I can't wait to see where your journey leads you.

Mom and Dad, thank you for showing me what forgiveness looks like. You have modeled humility, kindness, and love in some unbelievable situations. You have shown me that it is possible to let go of the hurts caused by others and trust in God's ultimate goodness in our lives and his control of the final outcomes. Dad, thank you for helping me believe in myself as a writer. Mom, thank you for your help with editing. My writing is clearer (and more proper) as a result. Your prayers have been much appreciated.

Thank you to all of you who trusted me with your stories of forgiveness. This book would not have been possible without you. You opened up your hearts to me and to everyone who reads this book. I pray that God will bless you with a harvest of rewards in his kingdom for helping to share his message of forgiveness.

Thank you to my siblings: Claire, Glenn, Paula, Gloria, and Linda, who encouraged me along the way.

To those who helped me navigate the maze of getting *490 Love: A Journey to Forgiveness* published:

Pastor Ben Dixon, thank you so much for your advice and encouragement. You helped me see the benefits of publishing this as a book, rather than as just a Bible study, and helped point me on my way to next steps in publishing.

Marge Mosher, thank you for your meticulous final editing. You did so much to help streamline the details and give my writing a final polish. You definitely helped me up my game.

Kelly L. Howard, thank you so much for taking a chance on a new author and for designing an unforgettable cover for this book. You are an exceptional artist, as well as a really down-to-earth and easy person to talk to.

Thank you to Karen Burkett and Shannon Herring at Christian Editing Services for helping to birth this baby. Your patience answering all of my questions has been much appreciated.

Introduction

When was the last time you opened up the Bible and read it as though it were God's instruction manual written especially for you? As though he meant what he said in his promises—and in his consequences? Have you hungered to read God's love letter to you? Have you believed that he can speak to you? That he wants to speak to you? Have you asked the Holy Spirit to bring God's Word to life in your daily walk with him? In your current circumstances? It will change your life!

God's Word is not an ancient manuscript. It is his living word to us. Today. Many people discount large portions of the Bible because they think that God hasn't kept up with the times and just doesn't understand the world that we now live in. Are you kidding? He is omniscient! He knows not only what happened in the past, but what will happen in the future. Besides, unlike us, God doesn't change his mind. He says, "I the Lord do not change..." (Malachi 3:6) Add to that the fact that we are not as original as we think. King Solomon, who is credited as being the wisest man that ever lived, said:

> What has been will be again, what has been done will be done again; there is nothing new under the sun.
>
> — ECCLESIASTES 1:9

Does God understand the "modern" society that we live in today? Does he understand the difficulties we face today as we seek to live a godly life? I assure you he does. Have you read much about ancient Roman civilization? About what life was like in Rome when Paul was imprisoned and writing his letters? Divorce was commonplace. There was little-to-no moral code. Much of the entertainment was based on violence. Not that much has changed...

God is still requiring that his people take up their crosses and follow him. He is still requiring that we die to our agenda so that we might live to his. God still expects us to forgive one another and love one another and follow his instruction manual. That's what *490 Love: A Journey to Forgiveness* is all about. You may be wondering why the title is *490 Love*. Well, one day Peter approached Jesus and asked him,

> "... 'Lord, how often should I forgive someone who sins against me? Seven times?'
>
> 'No, not seven times,' Jesus replied, 'but seventy times seven!'"
>
> — MATTHEW 18:21-22 NLT

Do a little math and you will discover that 70 x 7 equals 490. Jesus' love is a love that keeps on forgiving until it loses count of the offenses.

490 Love: A Journey to Forgiveness is about the Cross that poured out God's love on us and purchased our forgiveness. It's about surrender. It's about living our life God's way and according to his principles. It is about forgiving until we lose count, and loving without measure. It is about taking a look at the guidelines God gave us in his Word and applying them to our daily life. It is about finishing our race well.

Each chapter of *490 Love: A Journey to Forgiveness* will deal with a different layer of the forgiveness process while tying it into Biblical concepts to help secure the foundations of your Christian walk. Starting with Chapter 2, each chapter is broken into three parts. First, there is a lesson covering a foundational Biblical truth important to forgiving and loving others. Secondly, there is a real-life story for you to read where the lesson is applied. Last of all, discussion questions accompany each story along with a look at what the Bible says about the topic being highlighted. (These may be answered alone, with a friend, or in small discussion groups.) Finally, in the appendix there is a *Forgiveness Worksheet* that you may work through on your own as you choose to make things right with God and forgive others as he has forgiven you. Are you ready to get started?

What is Forgiveness?

Forgiveness is...

...one of the first words that draws us to Christ. When we hear the word FORGIVENESS we think of God's love for us. Knowing he sent his Son to die on a cross so that our sins would be paid for in full, blows our mind. We are told that God will forgive ANYTHING that we have done, no matter how horrible the sin. Even murder was covered by Calvary. When we repent and accept Christ's gift of forgiveness, we are born again and made new. We are filled with joy and love for our Savior because of the price that he paid on our behalf.

Forgiveness is...

...not a one-way street. What many of us Christians fail to realize is that yes, Christ died on the cross for us to forgive us of our sins—ALL of our sins, no matter how horrible. But, when we get saved, he expects us to take up our crosses too, and extend the same forgiveness and love that he gave us to those around us. Yes, we are supposed to forgive people for ANYTHING that they have done, no matter how horrible the sin—even murder—just as he forgave us. And it doesn't matter if the other person is sorry or not for what they have done. Christ forgave the soldiers who nailed him to the cross, and he forgave us long before we realized that we had sinned against him.

Forgiveness is...

...much easier to receive than it is to give. We want people who have sinned against us to know how horrible they are and to feel shame and regret for their actions. We want them to pay back what they have stolen from us. We want them to suffer like we have. Nothing would make us happier than to stand as judge and jury and condemn them to what we consider to be just payment for their actions. But that is not our job. It is God's. We show Jesus how much we value and appreciate his gift to us by paying it forward. The big things, the small things, the medium things—with his help we are called to love and to forgive them all.

Forgiveness is...

...a life-long journey. I don't presume to know everything that I need to know. Nor do I presume to always forgive as quickly or as completely as I should. I write this book because I am realizing how important forgiveness is to our Christian walk. I want to pass along some things that I have learned along my journey in hopes that it will help you as you continue along yours. On the following page is an acrostic that helps me remember the steps in forgiveness that God has been teaching me. My prayer is that as you read and apply the different steps, God will meet you. You will find freedom and healing when you extend to others the same forgiveness that he has extended to you. "For God so loved the world..." (John 3:16a).

7 Steps to Forgiveness

F Focus on God's grace and mercy and how much he has forgiven you.

O Offer the offense up to God and release it to him.

R Repent for any judgmental feelings or feelings of anger toward the person who offended you.

G Give thanks to God that he will bring good out of what happened.

I Invest in praying for the person who offended or hurt you.

V View the other person through God's eyes. He loves them!

E Erase the repetitive voice of the enemy from your thoughts by blessing the one who hurt you every time the person or situation comes to mind.

Chapter 1

The Cross: Where Love and Forgiveness Intersect

The Cross. Every Christian's race begins at the Cross. It is a symbol of death and of life. It is a symbol of unfathomable love and of unimaginable forgiveness. It is the crossroads where God meets us, redeems us, and transforms us. It is where love and forgiveness intersect.

The Cross cannot be denied, overlooked or forgotten by anyone who wishes to know God. It symbolizes the price he was willing to pay to have a relationship with us, and the price he expects us to pay if we want to have a relationship with him. The Cross is the point that connects heaven and earth. It connects our hearts to God's. "For God so loved the world that he gave his one and only Son, that whoever believes in him shall not perish but have eternal life" (John 3:16).

The problem? We are thankful that Jesus died for us on the Cross, but we forget that he requires us to take up our crosses, too. Jesus said to his disciples, "...Whoever wants to be my disciple must deny themselves and take up their cross and follow me. For whoever wants to save their life will lose it, but whoever loses their life for me will find it" (Matthew 16:24–25).

But he didn't really mean it, did he? I'm sure he didn't mean it, we reason with ourselves. However, Jesus clarifies, "Whoever does not take up their cross and follow me is not worthy of me. Whoever finds their life will lose it, and whoever loses their life for my sake will find it" (Matthew 10:38–39).

When Jesus wanted to make sure he got his point across, he would state both a commandment and its consequences. First Jesus commands us to take up our cross, and then he tells us the consequences if we don't. As we will see later in this book, he tells us to forgive, then tells us what will happen if we don't. He tells us to love, then tells us what will happen if we don't. In this case, if we don't take up our crosses, Jesus says that we are not worthy of him. We don't deserve him.

> **We are supposed to take the Cross with us.**

As Christians, many of us misunderstand the daily importance of the Cross. We tend to see it as a mile marker on our road to heaven. An important place, which we pause at briefly, before hurrying along our way. Meanwhile, we miss the point Jesus wanted to get across to us. We are supposed to take the Cross with us. Remember? Jesus said, "Whoever wants to be my disciple must deny themselves and take up their cross and follow me" (Matthew 16:24).

You see, the point of the Cross is SURRENDER. Permanent

surrender. Surrender of our plans. Surrender of our hopes. Surrender of our life. It's one of the most difficult things we will ever do. Jesus knows. He's been there. When he saw what God was requiring of him, he wanted to run from his cross too. His internal struggle was so intense that he sweat drops of blood. He prayed. He asked God to take away his cup of suffering—his cross—if at all possible. But he ultimately surrendered and said "Father... not my will, but yours be done" (Luke 22:42).

> **We try to mold and shape him into the kind of God we want to worship—instead of letting him mold and shape us.**

Have you surrendered? Have you given up trying to live life according to your own rules and plans? Have you surrendered your feelings and emotions to God? Your life and career plans? Have you died to you? Because God does things differently than we do. "'For my thoughts are not your thoughts, neither are your ways my ways,' declares the Lord" (Isaiah 55:8).

A humanistic mindset has so blinded many of us that we somehow think that we make the rules and God has to follow them. We try to mold and shape him into the kind of God we want to worship—instead of letting him mold and shape us. The cross is about surrender. It is about death. Death to our desires and our ambitions. Jesus calls us to deny ourselves, take up our cross and follow him (Matthew 16:24).

Paul said in Galatians, "I have been crucified with Christ and I no longer live, but Christ lives in me. The life I now live in the body, I live by faith in the Son of God, who loved me and gave himself for me" (Galatians 2:20). And just in case you're wondering if you really have to die, Paul goes on to say that we are "buried with him in baptism..." (Colossians 2:12). You don't bury someone unless they are dead. Getting saved and baptized is supposed to be the end of the *Dynasty of Self*. We are supposed to die so that Christ might live in us and through us. We are supposed to be new creations in Christ. As Paul said,

> ...he died for all, that those who live should no longer live for themselves but for him who died for them and was raised again.
>
> ...if anyone is in Christ, the new creation has come: The old has gone, the new is here!
>
> —2 CORINTHIANS 5:15 AND 17

We must carry our crosses with us so we don't forget. So we don't forget who we owe our lives to. So we don't forget the price of the love and forgiveness of our Lord and Savior.

In return, all Jesus asks is that we pay it forward—that we pass on that same love and forgiveness to others. He doesn't pretend that it will be easy or that it won't cost us anything. But we need to keep in mind that the reward he promises of eternity with him far surpasses any temporary discomfort and sacrifice that we may suffer now. He gave us his Word, the Bible, to show us the pathway we are to walk.

Forgiveness Story

My Forgiveness Journey

I didn't laugh much anymore. Biting sarcasm had replaced my sense of humor. I tried not to feel too much. I felt isolated. Unloved. I remember clearly the day that I knew that if something didn't change, the hurts, the bitterness and the anger would kill me. Literally. I could feel it eating at my core and consuming me. For a long time it had just been emotional, but now I could feel physical symptoms trying to attack my body. It scared me. I knew that cancer was circling and ready to devour the shell of me that was left.

I felt hopeless. It was obvious that I couldn't change my circumstances. I couldn't change the people around me. I resented those who hurt me. Those who were hurting the ones I loved. But I was powerless. I raged inside like a prisoner trapped under a life sentence. I should have been wearing a sign that said, *"Don't get too close, or a dose of acid might splash on you!"*

Yes, I was a Christian. Yes, I knew about forgiveness. But I also felt like people needed to pay. If they hurt me, they should hurt too. I wasn't a bad person—I was just reacting to those around me. They had hurt me. They had issues. They were to blame for the person that I was becoming. That's what I thought. What I believed.

If the people who hurt me were sorry, I would forgive them. The Bible said that I needed to. But they weren't sorry, so I was off the hook, right? I mean, surely God, who saw everything, understood. He couldn't expect me to take all the blame, could he? Then I found out that yes, he could. The day that I felt cancer attacking my body, trying to get a foothold, God and I had a chat. Strike that. More like God called me out and made several things very clear to me. The following were my takeaways:

1. **When I stand before God's Judgment Seat, he will be judging my actions on a stand-alone basis.** I am responsible for my actions *and my reactions*— regardless of what anyone else has done to me. Nobody else's actions will excuse me for mine. God will take care of others' actions when it's their turn to stand before him. What happens to them is none of my business. My actions and my actions alone are my business.

2. **God has called me to live life as an "action," not as a "reaction."** "Love your enemies"[1] is not a reaction. "Do good to them that hate you"[2] is not a reaction. "Bless them that curse you"[3] is not a reaction. Those are all commandments for action that Jesus gave to his disciples in the Sermon on the Mount. None of them are normal human reactions. God expects me to do the right thing and to follow his commandments, regardless of what anyone else around me is doing. "Hurt people, hurt people" is a short road to hell. Paul says that it is better to be wronged or cheated than to be suing (or perhaps holding grudges against?) our brothers and sisters (I Corinthians 6:7).

3. **It is not my responsibility to judge other people's actions.** I am not to judge, pay back, or try to exact vengeance for wrongs done to me. Those are all part of God's job—not mine. I have enough to take care of just trying to keep myself on track. People are a lot like icebergs. There is a lot more there than meets the eye. We interpret others' actions based on what we know, but the truth is that we know very little about even those closest to us. It is always a good idea to give others the benefit of the doubt and put the situation in God's hands. Trust him to make " ...all things work together for good..." (Romans 8:28 KJV).

4. **When I focus on my piece of the puzzle, God is free to do what he needs to with the other pieces.** Too often my attempts to fix things are counterproductive. I make things worse, rather than better—and get all uptight inside to boot! "Trust and obey,"[4] as the hymn says, is a good motto to stick to. I need to trust God and obey what he tells me to do! When I do my part, then he takes care of what I can't.

A seed was planted that day. No, there was not an overnight miracle difference in me, but there was a seed of new life germinating. Although it has been years, it is still a work in progress. I have had to go through the difficult process of developing new habit patterns. I have had to fight to overturn my normal reactions to circumstances and to ask God instead how he would have me act.

The change has been palpable, however, and I can see its ripple effects in those around me. Sometimes just one person changing can make a profound difference in a relationship. Forgiving those who have hurt me has unlocked the shackles that had me bound up. By freeing others, I freed myself. There is hope once again, and peace is becoming more of a normal part of my life.

This is a lifelong journey. There will always be new tests and trials and new circumstances that try my resolve to follow God and do things his way. But by his grace I will make the cut. The Bible says that it is God who works in us "both to will and to do of his good pleasure" (Philippians 2:13 KJV). When I can't do it on my own, he is there to carry me through.

It is my hope and prayer that you will be able to find the peace and freedom that you are seeking as you learn to forgive—whether it is God, others or even yourself that you are holding a grudge against. As you forgive, you will find God's love taking root in your heart. Then, instead of "acid," you will find love overflowing from you to those around you. That's the way of the Cross.

 Focus on God's grace and mercy and how much he has forgiven you.

Chapter 2

He Forgave It All! Have You?

We begin our forgiveness journey by focusing on God's grace and mercy and how much he has forgiven us. This is a vital part of our journey because it helps us keep things in proper perspective. When we realize how much God has forgiven us, and what our sins look like to him, the sins and trespasses that others have committed against us will seem small in comparison.

We also need to understand that if we don't forgive others, God won't forgive us. It's right there in the Sermon on the Mount—immediately after the Lord's Prayer: "For if you forgive other people when they sin against you, your heavenly Father will also forgive you. But if you do not forgive others their sins, your Father will not forgive your sins" (Matthew 6:14–15). Could God really mean that? If I don't forgive other people then God won't forgive me?!? You've got to be kidding! God is love, right? He forgives everything, right? Let's take a look at the parable that Jesus told of The Unforgiving Servant and find out.

The Parable of the Unforgiving Servant

Therefore, the kingdom of heaven is like a king who wanted to settle accounts with his servants. As he began the settlement, a man who owed him ten thousand bags of gold was brought to him. Since he was not able to pay, the master ordered that he and his wife and his children and all that he had be sold to repay the debt.

At this the servant fell on his knees before him. 'Be patient with me,' he begged, 'and I will pay back everything.' The servant's master took pity on him, canceled the debt and let him go.

But when that servant went out, he found one of his fellow servants who owed him a hundred silver coins. He grabbed him and began to choke him. 'Pay back what you owe me!' he demanded. His fellow servant fell to his knees and begged him, 'Be patient with me, and I will pay it back.' But he refused. Instead, he went off and had the man thrown into prison until he could pay the debt.

When the other servants saw what had happened, they were outraged and went and told their master everything that had happened. Then the master called the servant in. 'You wicked servant,' he said, 'I canceled all that debt of yours because you begged me to. Shouldn't you have had mercy on your fellow servant just as I had on you?' In anger his master handed him over to the jailers to be tortured, until he should pay back all he owed.

This is how my heavenly Father will treat each of you unless you forgive your brother or sister from your heart.

—MATTHEW 18:23–35

I don't know about you, but my initial impression of this parable was that it was basically a nice fairy tale story about a king and a mean servant who was suitably punished. But a parable by definition is a comparison or analogy. It is usually a short, simple story dealing with a topic that the audience is familiar with. It is told in hopes of teaching them a lesson. As I reread this story, did a little studying, and put it into context, I was blown away! Let me break the story down and share with you what I learned. Let's start at the beginning.

> Therefore, the kingdom of heaven is like a king who wanted to settle accounts with his servants. As he began the settlement, a man who owed him ten thousand bags of gold was brought to him.
>
> —MATTHEW 18:23-24

At the time when Jesus told this story, kings were common rulers. We could substitute *Governor* or *President* here. For the people that Jesus was talking to, this was not a fairy tale, but a story that they could relate to. They knew the same type of thing could happen to them. In the kingdom of heaven, Jesus is the King and we as Christians are his servants. So, as Jesus is settling accounts with his servants, he finds out that one of his servants owes him ten thousand bags of gold. Now the actual Greek says "ten thousand talents," but either way, it somehow translated into ten thousand dollars in my head. Figure in some inflation and I supposed it might even be as much as one hundred thousand dollars—or maybe even a million dollars—a lot of money for anyone, but still a debt that could be repaid.

However, a little research revealed that the Greek word *myriōn*[5] used in this passage for 10,000 by extension means "innumerably many"[6] and a talent of gold "was about 180,000 days' wages, often implying a vast, unattainable sum."[7] Jesus was making it exceedingly clear to all who heard him that this was an enormous, unpayable debt. If you do the actual math, you end up with 1,800,000,000 or 1 billion, 800 million days' wages. There was NO WAY the servant could ever repay that kind of money.

> Since he was not able to pay, the master ordered that he and his wife and his children and all that he had be sold to repay the debt.
>
> At this the servant fell on his knees before him. 'Be patient with me,' he begged, 'and I will pay back everything.'
>
> —MATTHEW 18:25–26

In light of what we learned about the actual size of the debt, I would daresay that the servant was somewhat naïve. He didn't offer to repay what he could. He told the king that he would repay ALL that money. How could he ever expect to pay back that kind of debt? It was impossible! (Just like it would be impossible for us to ever repay God for the debt that he has forgiven us. We can't *earn* our salvation!) Back then, there was no such thing as declaring bankruptcy and getting some or all of your debt wiped off the books. If you couldn't repay a debt, you were thrown into debtor's prison along with your entire family, or sold into slavery, until the debt was repaid—which in this case meant FOREVER. That actually happened to people whose debt was large enough.

(Good thing the rules have changed for us, huh?) But this guy was really lucky!

> The servant's master took pity on him, canceled the debt and let him go.
>
> —MATTHEW 18:27

When the servant begged for mercy, the king did not throw the impossibility of ever repaying the debt back at the servant and laugh at him. Instead he forgave him...*the entire amount!* Just as God has forgiven us our inconceivable, unrepayable, debt of sin... without rubbing our faces in it. Wow! I bet the guy was really excited and grateful to the king. I know I would have been! I mean he and his entire family were saved from spending the rest of their lives in prison or as slaves! But what...?

> But when that servant went out, he found one of his fellow servants who owed him a hundred silver coins. He grabbed him and began to choke him. 'Pay back what you owe me!' he demanded. His fellow servant fell to his knees and begged him, 'Be patient with me, and I will pay it back.' But he refused. Instead, he went off and had the man thrown into prison until he could pay the debt.
>
> — MATTHEW 18:28–30

He did what? My first reaction was to judge the servant self-righteously and to say "How could you do such a thing?" A hundred silver coins, according to my research, is 100 denarii in the Greek, or 100 days' wages[8]—a very manageable sum. Why couldn't the servant forgive that little bit after all that the king had forgiven him?

Then I realized that I act the very same way all the time. How many people have I been unwilling to forgive for slighting me in some insignificant way? The coworker who lied about me behind my back to the boss... The relative who criticized how I was raising my children... The stranger who cut me off in traffic...

It is so easy to hold grudges against people! The only way we can truly forgive the way God wants us to is to take our focus off how others have wronged us and put our focus back on how much God loves us and has forgiven us—far more than we could ever repay. Like we so often do, the Unforgiving Servant did not appreciate the amazing gift that he had been given. A few people noticed his ungrateful behavior:

> When the other servants saw what had happened, they were outraged and went and told their master everything that had happened. Then the master called the servant in. 'You wicked servant,' he said, 'I canceled all that debt of yours because you begged me to.'
>
> —MATTHEW 18:31–32

Didn't we beg him to forgive us, too? Didn't he do it?

> 'Shouldn't you have had mercy on your fellow servant just as I had on you?'
>
> — MATTHEW 18:33

Shouldn't we? Jesus DIED to forgive us of our sins. ALL of our sins. The least we can do is forgive our fellow Christians when they commit sins against us. Right? But ultimately God leaves the choice up to us. However, he makes it clear that if we choose not to forgive, there will be consequences...

> In anger his master handed him over to the jailers to be tortured, until he should pay back all he owed.
>
> —MATTHEW 18:34

This is the verse that we all want to skip over. We have already established that the servant would never be able to repay his debt—which means that his torture will now last forever. Forever is a long time to be tortured. In my mind, ten seconds is a long time to be tortured! How could a loving God do such a thing? Did I misread something? No, the next verse states it very clearly;

> This is how my heavenly Father will treat each of you unless you forgive your brother or sister from your heart.
>
> —MATTHEW 18:35

From your heart... If you believe as I do that the Bible is the infallible Word of God, then this is a part of the instruction manual that we don't want to skip over. Not forgiving *from our heart* puts us on a detour to hell? Yes, but only if *we* choose it.

To avoid this detour, all we have to do is forgive our Christian brothers and sisters the way we have been forgiven. Yes, I said our fellow Christians. That is what the Bible says. Did you notice earlier that it said it was one of the man's *fellow servants* that he had thrown into prison? I think God wants that to be our starting point for forgiveness. First and foremost, we must forgive our fellow Christians. However, if you are anything like me, you find those people are the hardest to forgive most of the time, because *they should know better.* However, let's face it. We all should know better! Besides, this is not an optional item on the checklist. We must forgive if we want to be forgiven by God.

We must forgive if we want to be forgiven by God.

Remember, if we decide not to forgive our fellow servants, then God will not forgive us. Not because he is mean or anything, but because those are the consequences of our choice not to forgive. We get to choose our own outcome. It makes sense, really. Can you imagine heaven with a bunch of people who can't forgive each other? Sounds like hell to me—Oh, wait! It is! Can we afford not to forgive our brothers? I know I can't! Whatever they have done to me is not worth spending eternity in hell over.

Forgiveness Story

My Daily Cross

Tall and handsome like his daddy, Shane is a pleasure to have as a son. He is respectful, obedient, helpful, kind, smart, and loves to sing. Only God knows how often I pause during the day and thank him for giving my husband and me the perfect son for us. Few people would understand—or even believe me if I told them.

You see, Shane was diagnosed with autism as a young child. At one point my husband Trey and I were uncertain if he would ever speak—but he did. We were unsure if he would ever be potty-trained—but he was. We wondered if he would ever be able to handle regular schoolwork—yet he can.

So many worries, so much work, so many hurdles—you probably thought raising Shane was my cross. No, Shane is my son. Although it has not always been easy, helping him learn and grow is always a pleasure. No, I would not consider Shane to be my cross. I doubt there is another soul alive who loves me like Shane does. There is no one who forgives me as readily or who brings me such joy on a daily basis.

No, my cross has to do with your perfect children, children who are growing up in Christian homes with Christian parents who go to church every week, yet who exclude my son at church events. Children who can speak their minds without difficulty, who are popular and have so many friends that they can't find time for all of them—yet they don't seem to have the time to say hi to Shane. Children who look the other way when he walks by. Children who invite everyone but Shane to their parties. Yes, forgiving your children is my cross.

Why? My son has to work hard to speak, yet he will introduce himself to your children. He will try to have a conversation with them, only to have them brush past him at times and walk away. Shane will invite them over to play, only to be rebuffed. Sometimes when he says his stomach hurts after one of these incidents (he never calls your children names or gets mad at them), my stomach hurts too... I smile and tell him how proud I am of him. I tell him that he did the right thing to invite them, but that not everyone will be his friend. I tell him that I love him.

I often struggle to forgive you, too. When you steer your children away from my son or come up with lame excuses explaining why they can't come to his birthday party—as though he had some fatal, contagious disease. You know, my son doesn't bite, scratch, kick, or fight. You will never hear him curse or call anyone names. He is probably one of the most kind and polite young men out there. Don't you see his big heart? I want to shake you sometimes and say, "Don't you know that Jesus loves my son Shane? If Jesus walked the earth today, I know he would have time to spend with him. He would love him! Don't you know what Jesus said in Matthew 25:40? 'Truly I tell you, whatever you did for one of the least of these brothers and sisters of mine, you did for me.'"

Yes, my daily cross is forgiving you and your children. It's hard for me most days. I want to hold grudges and be mad at your lack of compassion. I want to yell at you and your children. With all that you have been given, couldn't you give back a few minutes here and there? A smile, a high-five, or an "It's so nice to see you today!" would make Shane so happy. A real friend would mean so much to him...

Having a good attitude and being kind to people who are unkind to Shane is a heavy cross to bear some days. I smile for Shane and try to shield him. I don't want him to become bitter or hard. I make excuses to him for you—and then cry when he is not around to see.

I can really relate to the passage where Peter asks Jesus, "Lord, how many times shall I forgive my brother or sister who sins against me? Up to seven times?" (Matthew 18:21b). I mean, the Jewish teachers of the law of Peter's day said that three times was plenty. Seven is more than double that! For me, those first seven times can seem like more than I can handle sometimes. But Jesus answered Peter and said, "I tell you, not seven times, but seventy times seven" (Matthew 18:22).

You see, Jesus knew that most of us can easily keep mental track of seven grievances, after which we would happily start our Trespass Tally Sheet to keep track of how much others have hurt us. The mental count when we follow his way, however, starts getting murky long before we reach 490. The result is a habit of forgiveness rather than a pattern of holding grudges.

Don't worry, I do understand. If I am totally honest, I have to admit that I would probably be you if my son had been born differently. When I judge you, I am judging myself. I am not perfect either. There are women who really need friends that I pass by sometimes without reaching out. I also choose my friends many times based on how they make me feel about myself, instead of focusing on the other person's need for acceptance and love. I also am more likely to hang out with people who are similar to me, because I find that to be more comfortable. "The least of these" are not always on my short list of people to reach out to. And yes, I am reminded of some of Jesus' other words, such as "Let any one of you who is without sin be the first to throw a stone" (John 8:7).

Jesus and Shane are teaching me to stretch my horizons. They are teaching me the value of every human being. In the Sermon on the Mount Jesus said, "pray for them which despitefully use you" (Matthew 5:44 KJV). So I am learning to pray for some of you when I feel that you are treating Shane poorly. I hope that you are praying for me too when I mess up! Jesus loves us all, and he died for all of our sins. His sacrificial love gives me the strength to keep moving forward in forgiveness. It helps me "do unto others as I would have others do unto me"[9]—and my son. With Jesus beside me and his love growing in my heart, my daily cross is getting easier to bear.

My Daily Cross

After reading **My Daily Cross**, answer the following questions thoughtfully:

1. How did this story make you feel?

2. Do you relate more to the author of this story or to the people she needs to forgive? Why?

3. Perhaps your life circumstances are different, but do you have a *daily cross* of your own? Is it possible that at times you are guilty of doing the same thing to others that you are judging them for?

4. Why does God command us to forgive people who are acting in an obviously unchristian manner?

5. Did reading this story change your perspective or the way you will act in the future? How?

What does the Bible have to say?

Let's see what scripture has to say about how we should act towards those who treat us poorly—either intentionally or unintentionally.

1 Peter 3:8-9
Finally, all of you, be like-minded, be sympathetic, love one another, be compassionate and humble. Do not repay evil with evil or insult with insult. On the contrary, repay evil with blessing, because to this you were called so that you may inherit a blessing.

1. Why would Peter command his readers to be "like-minded" when everyone is so different? Is that actually possible for us? If so, how?

2. When it says "do not repay evil with evil or insult with insult," is Peter telling us to *act* or to *react* in our interactions with others? Why is this important for us as Christians?

3. Does anyone come to mind when you think of being personally insulted or treated in an evil manner? How can you bless that person this week? Be specific—with the action, not the person.

Leviticus 19:18
Do not seek revenge or bear a grudge against anyone among your people, but love your neighbor as yourself. I am the Lord.

1. What does it mean to "bear a grudge?" Do you bear any grudges at the moment?

2. How are we to love our neighbor? Do you remember who Jesus said our neighbor was? (Think the parable of The Good Samaritan).

Romans 12:4–5
For just as each of us has one body with many members, and these members do not all have the same function, so in Christ we, though many, form one body, and each member belongs to all the others.

1. What happens in the human body if different body parts reject one another? Can we reject one another in the Body of Christ without hurting ourselves?

PRAYER

Father God, thank you first and foremost that you loved me even when I was your enemy. Thank you that you forgave my sins even when I didn't deserve your pardon. I ask that you would shed your love abroad in my heart and help me to love those who don't treat me, or those I love, the way you would have them treat us. Lord, please bless them and love them and make your heart known to them. Please forgive them for their actions and help me to forgive them the way that you have forgiven me. When I am tempted to judge, open my eyes to my own shortcomings so that I may have mercy on the shortcomings of others. I ask these things in Jesus' name. Amen.

Memory Verse:

Choose one of the previous passages that you would like to learn and make a part of your spiritual arsenal. Copy it down using your preferred Bible translation and memorize it.

_____

_____

_____

_____

_____

F

O Offer the offense up to God and release it to him.

R

G

I

V

E

Chapter 3

Put Off the Old...
Put On the New

We are now ready to take the second step in our forgiveness journey. After gaining a better understanding of the parable of The Unforgiving Servant, I hope that you not only appreciate the magnitude of God's forgiveness in your own life, but also understand the importance of extending that same forgiveness towards others. Remember, all that Jesus asks of us in return is that we pay it forward, extending the same love and forgiveness to others that he so freely gave to us at Calvary.

In this chapter we will focus on offering offenses up to God and releasing them to him. Did you know that as long as we hold on to the grudges and the offenses that have been committed against us, God is unable to forgive us? He is also unable to replace them with his love, joy and peace. Which is better? To hold on tightly to unforgiveness, or to release it in exchange for God's better plan for our life?

Picture, if you will, a beggar child from a large city in a third world country. This child lives on the street and is filthy, covered in sores, and starving. They are used to scrounging through garbage heaps and begging in order to survive. Violence and pain are daily reminders that no one cares about them, loves them, or will protect them.

One day everything changes. The beggar child is rescued off the streets and offered a new life. They're offered all the food they can eat and a safe, warm place to sleep at night. They're offered clean, new clothes. They're offered love and the chance to be part of a family. They're offered security, hope, and a future.

However, the beggar child must be willing to pay the price. It's a high price. You see, the child must give up their old way of life. They must surrender their dirty rags. They must be willing to be bathed—regularly. They must give up their right to do what they want, when they want. They must be willing to follow another's rules… The choice may seem obvious to us, but there is a real sacrifice involved for the child. For some the cost would be too high. The change, too dramatic. They will choose to stay on the streets.

What would you choose if you were that child? What are you choosing today? God has offered to adopt you into his family and love you. He will provide for you, protect you, and give you hope and a future—not only in this life, but for all eternity. But you, too, must be prepared to make some sacrifices…

Today we are going to talk about putting off the old and putting on the new. When you became a Christian, you were adopted into a new family and you became a child of God's. He is your Father now. Paul said it well in his letter to the Ephesians:

> ...you have heard about him and were taught in him, as the truth is in Jesus, **to put off your old self, which belongs to your former manner of life** and is corrupt through deceitful desires, and to be renewed in the spirit of your minds, and **to put on the new self, created after the likeness of God** in true righteousness and holiness.
>
> —EPHESIANS 4:21–24 ESV (Emphasis mine)

Paul is telling the Ephesians, that just like the beggar child who is offered a new life, they need to put off their "old self" which belonged to their former manner of life. In exchange, they need to put on their "new self" that God created in his own likeness, in righteousness and holiness.

When we put on our new self, we begin to look like our Father, and people will start to notice the family resemblance. Since you gave your life to Christ has there been a change in how you live? Do you do things differently than you did before? When people look at you do they see a change? Do they see Jesus?

Maybe "putting off the old self" and "putting on the new self" sound like great ideas, but what do they mean exactly? Let's skip down a few verses to where Paul gets a bit more specific about what we need to put off, or as he states here, get rid of: "Get rid of all bitterness, rage and anger, brawling and slander, along with every form of malice" (Ephesians 4:31). Okay, so most of those sound pretty bad. I can see why we, as Christians, should not be behaving that way. However, it is also easy to skip over these words lightly and not really focus on what it means to get rid of these things in our lives. To help us meditate a bit on what Paul means here, I am going to go over the definitions of these words. You may be surprised to find out what these words actually imply practically speaking in your life.

The first word on our list is *bitterness*. Let's take a look at its definition in *Webster's New World Dictionary*, along with other related definitions that will help us understand what Paul is saying.

> **Bitter/Bitterness**: ...characterized by strong feelings of hatred, resentment, cynicism, etc.
>
> (Related definitions:)
>
> **Resentment**: a feeling of bitter hurt or indignation, from a sense of being injured or offended.
>
> **Cynical**: believing that people are motivated in all their actions only by selfishness; denying the sincerity of people's motives and actions...[10]

Do you ever really dislike people? Do you ever feel hurt or indignant about how someone has treated you? Do you get offended easily? Do you deny the sincerity of people's *good intentions*? Do you think that most people are selfish and act accordingly? All of a sudden bitterness is something that we can all relate to on a daily basis... perhaps a little too well. But God wants us to put off bitterness. It is not one of his characteristics and should not be one of the characteristics of his children.

Next we have *rage* and *anger*, which I am going to group together since they are close cousins. However, I am going to reverse their order since I believe that anger is a precursor to rage. If you give in to anger and feed it, then it develops into rage...

> **Anger:** a feeling of displeasure resulting from injury, mistreatment, opposition, etc. and usually showing itself in a desire to fight back at the supposed cause of this feeling... SYN—**anger** is broadly applicable to feelings of resentful or revengeful displeasure... **rage** suggests a violent outburst of anger in which self-control is lost.
>
> **Rage:** insanity; ...a furious uncontrolled anger; esp., a brief spell of raving fury.[11]

Do you ever feel unhappy because you think that you have been mistreated? Do you ever want to fight back or pay back someone who has hurt or mistreated you? Do you want revenge? That is anger. If you give in to those feelings long enough, you will find yourself losing control. Now your emotions are controlling you. That is rage, an anger that controls you instead of vice versa. If not reined in, rage can eventually lead to murder. If we fight anger when it first starts to set in—when we just feel that irritated ping in our heart when we think about our offender—we will avoid even starting down that destructive path. Remember, we are God's children and have been adopted into his family. We should act accordingly.

The next two things that we need to get rid of are ones that at first glance you may think don't apply to you—*brawling* and *slander*. Let's read their definitions as they apply to our passage to better understand what they mean in our lives:

Brawl: ...a rough, noisy, quarrel or fight; row...

Slander: the utterance in the presence of another person of a false statement or statements, damaging to a third person's character or reputation...[12]

Brawling doesn't just happen in bar rooms. Have you ever had a noisy quarrel? I know I have. What about slandering? Is it possible that when you "catch up" with your friends, you are repeating something that may not be true and that may damage someone else's reputation? God wants us to control our emotions *and* our actions—especially when it comes to our mouths. Remember, we are representing the family name and people are watching us. Do you represent the life of a child of God? Is his character reflected in your actions?

Our last word is *malice*. I always think of criminals and *malice aforethought* when I hear this word, but malice is something that I think we are all guilty of at one time or another.

Malice: active ill will; desire to harm another or to do mischief; spite... SYN. – **malice** implies a deep-seated animosity that delights in causing others to suffer or in seeing them suffer... **Spite** suggests a mean desire to hurt, annoy, or frustrate others, usually as displayed in petty, vindictive acts...[13]

Maybe you would never hurt another person, but does seeing someone else hurt ever make you happy? Do you justify your feelings because *they had it coming to them*? *They deserved to suffer*? Do you like to annoy people who have annoyed you? Or perhaps you engage in petty acts to get even with them? These actions all belong to the same family—and it's not God's. We will discuss later in this book about how we are always serving one master or another. You either choose God's way, or by default you are choosing Satan's. It may sound harsh, but it's true. Put off the old you and put on the new you!

I know. It's not that easy. I was painfully reminded of this recently when my feelings were trampled on by some people I had known for a long time. I didn't like how they acted towards me, and I thought that they were being selfish and rude. Resentment and anger and perhaps a touch of spite were clamoring to be heard. You know, I had to pray (repeatedly) and ask God to nail those feelings to the cross. At the time, it hurt that much to surrender my feelings. I felt like I was having to die inside to my rights, my feelings, my desires. It's not easy to "deny ourselves, take up our cross and follow..." (adapted from Matthew 16:24). But, there was no way to go forward and maintain the relationships in peace if I didn't. Surrendering my hurts was painful. I felt that I had the right to my feelings, but I knew that I couldn't afford to hold on to them. The price would be too great.

> **God just asks us to obey. We don't have to feel like it when we do.**

After I surrendered my feelings to God, I began to ask God to bless those who had hurt me. I am not going to lie. I was still very angry when I started praying for them. I didn't *feel* like blessing them. To be honest, my attitude was horrible to begin with. But God just asks us to obey. We don't have to feel like it when we do. Does a child have to *feel* like taking out the trash or cleaning their room or do they just need to obey their parents and do it? What is neat about God, is that as we do what he has asked us to do, he takes care of the feelings.

It took about 24 hours for my peace to fully return, but it did. The other parties may never know how much it cost me to be gracious and kind under the circumstances, but that doesn't matter. God does. Every time that I obey him and choose his way the process gets easier.

So, now that we have discarded our old rags, let's take a look at the new clothes that God wants us to put on. In Ephesians 4, Paul says that after we get rid of bitterness, rage, anger, brawling, slander, and malice, we are to "be kind and compassionate to one another, forgiving each other, just as in Christ God forgave [us]" (Ephesians 4:32). Once we put off the old, the new is so much easier to put on. When you are no longer angry and spiteful, it is much easier to be kind and compassionate and forgive others. This takes us back to our first lesson about always being mindful of how much God has forgiven us.

Remember that really important concepts in the Bible are often repeated. Paul wrote to the Colossian church, "But now you must also rid yourselves of all such things as these: anger, rage, malice, slander, and filthy language from your lips" (Colossians 3:8). Sound familiar? He continues in verse 10, "...and have put on the new self, which is being renewed in knowledge in the image of its Creator." I like to think of *renewed* as being made new again. We are being recreated in the image of our Creator. Doesn't that blow your mind?

After we have taken off the old ways of doing things, then Paul tells us what to put on or *clothe ourselves with*:

> Therefore, as God's chosen people, holy and dearly loved, clothe yourselves with compassion, kindness, humility, gentleness and patience. Bear with each other and forgive one another if any of you has a grievance against someone. Forgive as the Lord forgave you. And over all these virtues put on love, which binds them all together in perfect unity.
>
> —COLOSSIANS 3:12–14

Our new articles of clothing now include not only compassion and kindness, but also humility, gentleness, and patience.

Humility is an especially important item in our wardrobe. It is the counterpart to pride in the devil's wardrobe. You see it is usually our pride that gets us angry with others and makes us desire revenge. Humility, in contrast, will help us put others' needs above our own—their feelings above ours—thus enabling us to forgive any wrongdoing that has been done to us.

> **It is usually our pride that gets us angry with others and makes us desire revenge.**

Once again Paul talks about forgiving as the Lord forgave us, but he adds the need to bear with one another. Have you ever said that you *can't bear to have someone around*? Well, God says you must. He says "bear with each other..." (Colossians 3:13a). So, how do we do this? The key is in the next verse where he says, "And over all these virtues put on love, which binds them all together in perfect unity" (Colossians 3:14). Remember, the Cross is where love and forgiveness intersect. You can't have true forgiveness without love, nor can you have true love without forgiveness. They are dependent one upon the other. As Paul says, love binds together in perfect unity all the other virtues listed in verses 12 and 13. It is also what binds us all together in unity as the Body of Christ.

Remember that the second step in our forgiveness journey is offering up our offenses to God. We have to put off the old to make room for the new. When you offer offenses up to God, you are in fact saying: *God, I renounce my old life and my old way of doing things. I choose you. I choose to be part of your family. Please clothe me in your forgiveness and your love. Make me more like you.*

Forgiveness Story

The Choice

Choose not to take offense... The words that the pastor had spoken this past Sunday resonated in my mind. It was now Tuesday, and today I was in the mood to take offense. Ha! The mechanic was trying to rip us off and I was not about to let him.

Just three weeks ago this same mechanic had checked our brakes and said that they were fine, and now he was claiming that the awful shuddering that our car had been doing ever since his recent $1,350 repair was not caused by anything that he had messed up, but by the brakes. This guy was unbelievable! Does he think that I am an idiot? No, I'm not a mechanic, but *his shop* had just checked our brakes and told us that they were fine. And now they wanted another $350 of our hard-earned (and tightly pinched) dollars!

My husband Pierre, ever the "err on the side of safety and caution" guy, thought that we should go ahead and get the brakes fixed like the mechanic was suggesting, but I was unconvinced. Mechanics had tried (and I'm sure succeeded at times) to rip me off before. As a profession they were on my list of people to watch out for and distrust.

Choose not to take offense... Seriously? How could I not? Especially after my conversation with said mechanic. Since I was the one who drove the car most often during the week, my husband agreed that perhaps I should explain to the mechanic what the car had been doing on hills since we had gotten it back from the shop. I also felt it was my duty to inform the mechanic that we really couldn't afford to have more repair work done at the moment and that *he had said that the brakes were fine just three week before!* Really? Now they were not?! (Of course, I said all of this in my nicest, *I just don't understand how this could be*, voice).

In an effort to show me that he understood how I felt (as if!!), the mechanic proceeded to tell me that he and his family had recently had to pay $2,000 for furnace repairs, $500 for a new washer and were in need of a new car themselves. He "understood" not being able to afford expensive repairs and feeling vulnerable when you don't know a whole lot about the problem in question. Yada, yada, yada. His plan to calm me down backfired on him, because all I could think was, *Well, with the bill from this next repair you'll have $1,700 of our money. One or two more repairs and we'll have single-handedly paid off all of your repair bills for you!*

Choose not to take offense... Ok. There was the off chance that the mechanic was telling the truth. That a closer look at the inner workings of the brakes had revealed something that a routine inspection had not. It was possible that there was no reason to take offense at all. Could I afford to waste my energy and health being mad over something that could just as easily be a figment of my imagination?

Ok, God. I surrender. All of our money belongs to you and you have always taken care of us and supplied our needs. I will not live in fear and worry and anger. I choose to trust you. You are the Judge, not me. Please forgive me. I ask that you would bless our mechanic and his family. It would seem that he has been through some tough times himself recently. Please provide the money that his family needs. If they need a new car, please provide that for them as well. (If you want to give us a new car at the same time, that would be fine too...) I just pray blessing on them. I thank you for the new brakes that we are getting and I thank you for keeping my family safe. I choose not to take offense today. Instead I choose to bless. Thank you, God, for your Holy Spirit enabling me to do the right thing. I choose life, and I choose your way. Amen.

I did have to repeat that prayer a couple of times when my blood pressure started to climb again, but soon I meant every word. And you know what? The resentment dissipated like fog on a sunny day.

The Choice

After reading **The Choice,** answer the following questions thoughtfully:

1. How often do you find yourself feeling upset over real (or possibly imagined) offenses? Hourly? Daily? Weekly? How much of your time is caught up in these types of thoughts?

2. When you allow yourself to be easily offended, who is at the center of your attention? Who should be?

3. Why is it important *not* to let your mind dwell on these types of thoughts? What/Who should you be focusing your attention on instead?

4. In **The Choice,** it was worry about money and concern about being lied to that were at the root of the offense. What do you find is at the root of most of the things that bother or offend you? Fear? Lack of trust in God? Pride? Something else? Are these traits that you want to multiply in your life?

5. How do you think that your life will improve by choosing not to take offense? How will you feel differently? Give concrete examples if possible.

What does the Bible have to say?

Let's see what scripture has to say about offenses and how we are supposed to react when they come.

Luke 17:1 NKJV
Then He (Jesus) said to the disciples, "It is impossible that no offenses should come..." (Clarification mine.)

1. What does Jesus say is the percent of possibility that offenses will come?

Luke 17:4 (Jesus is continuing the above conversation).
Even if they (your brother or sister) ***sin against you seven times in a day and seven times come back to you saying 'I repent,' you must forgive them."*** (Clarification mine.)

1. How would you feel if someone sinned against you seven times in one day and kept coming back saying that they were sorry?

2. Does Jesus suggest or command that we forgive them each time? By forgiving them repeatedly, what godly traits are we developing?

Proverbs 19:11 (ESV)
Good sense makes one slow to anger, and it is his glory to overlook an offense.

1. Repeatedly in the Bible God is described as "slow to anger and abounding in steadfast love."[14] Is it possible for us to follow in God's footsteps? How?

2. What is the definition of *glory* in this context? Look it up.

Proverbs 17:9
Whoever would foster love covers over an offense, but whoever repeats the matter separates close friends.

1. How can we "cover over an offense" in love? Why should we? What happens within the church when we don't? Who wins and who loses?

PRAYER

Father God, I thank you that you sent your Son Jesus to earth, to live here among us as a man. I thank you that he understands all about offenses and knows personally what they feel like. Help me bring any offenses that have been committed against me and lay them down at the foot of the Cross. Help me to forgive—repeatedly, if necessary. Help me to be slow to anger and quick to overlook any offenses that are committed against me. I want to foster love and not division. Help me to put off my old self which belongs to my former way of life and put on the new self which was created in your image. I want to become more like you. Thank you for hearing me and answering my prayer. In Jesus' name I pray. Amen.

Memory Verse:

Choose one of the previous passages that you would like to learn and make a part of your spiritual arsenal. Copy it down using your preferred Bible translation and memorize it.

_____

_____

_____

_____

_____

FORGIVE

Repent for any judgmental feelings or feelings of anger toward the person who offended you.

Chapter 4

Mercy Triumphs Over Judgment[15]

We are now ready to take the third step in our forgiveness journey. We have learned the importance of focusing our attention on how much God has forgiven us, rather than how much others have offended or hurt us. We have also seen how vital it is to offer any offenses up to God and release them to him.

Now we will confront the need to repent of any judgmental feelings or feelings of anger toward the person who offended us or transgressed against us. This third step is a crucial part of our forgiveness journey. We can't forgive others when we are stuck in judgment mode. When we release offenses to God, that includes releasing to God the right to judge the perpetrator. After all, that is his job, not ours.

Look at it this way. A friend asks you to go to court with him because he caught his neighbor stealing from him and he is suing the neighbor. You agree to meet him at the courthouse. On the day of the trial, you walk into the courtroom and see your friend sitting up front with the prosecuting attorney. He waves at you, and you take a seat to wait for the trial to start.

As you wait your mind wanders. Then you hear the gavel strike calling the court to order, but when you look up, your jaw drops open. Your friend has gotten tired of waiting for the judge to arrive and do his job and has climbed up into the judge's seat and is banging the gavel. When the courtroom gets quiet, he proceeds to tell his neighbor that he sentences him to five years in jail for stealing from him.

The bailiff promptly intervenes with some handcuffs and hauls your friend out of court. How is this going to end for your friend? Needless to say, not well. Most likely your friend will be found in contempt of court when the judge arrives and will be fined or even have to serve time himself. Why? He is not the judge. That's not his job. He doesn't have the right or the authority to pass sentence on his neighbor. He is a witness and a plaintiff, but that is it.

Seems obvious, doesn't it? But how often do you and I try to stand and pass judgment on our brothers or sisters who have offended us or sinned against us? We are not the judge. God is. Psalm 50:6 says, "for God himself is judge."[16] Psalm 75:7 says, "It is God who judges: he brings one down, he exalts another." We see this fact stated repeatedly all throughout the Bible.

Our problem is that we get our roles mixed up. You see, we are witnesses to many things, but witnesses don't judge cases. They don't have enough information to make a just and fair decision. That is the job of the judge. The judge has all of the pertinent facts needed to mete out justice. When someone offends us or hurts us, we as witnesses may report what we have seen to the Judge. As plaintiffs we may tell him what has happened to us, but then we need to let the situation go.

In Isaiah 3:13 we read, "The Lord takes his place in court; he rises to judge the people." God will decide if any punishment needs to be meted out. He is the judge, and that is his job, not ours. Later, in Jeremiah 17:10 we read, "I the Lord search the heart, and examine the mind, to reward each person according to their conduct, according to what their deeds deserve." Can you or I "search the heart" or "examine the mind?" No, of course not. We need to loosen our stranglehold on the offenses that have been committed against us and trust that God knows what he is doing. He will judge each person "according to what their deeds deserve" (Jeremiah 17:10b). Letting go of the desire to judge or punish others is necessary for us to be able to forgive them from our hearts.

Sometimes, instead of judging others, we decide that we just want to prosecute or accuse them. However, that is not our role either. You see, in Revelation we read that Satan is the accuser of our brothers and sisters (Revelation 12:10). He is the prosecutor. He is constantly making sure that God knows who has messed up and fallen short of perfection in any way. He presents cases, hoping to get us punished and locked up forever. Do you want to be on his team? If not, remember, we are not the judge, nor the prosecutor. We are merely witnesses.

The wonderful thing for us, is that if we end up in God's court as a defendant (perhaps for being in contempt of court and trying to impersonate a judge), we have a wonderful defense attorney. Jesus is our advocate with the Father (1 John 2:1). 1 Timothy 2:5 says that there is one mediator between God and us, and that is Jesus. When you repent for your judgmental feelings towards others, Jesus will intervene with God on your behalf and you will be forgiven. However, remember that God says that he won't forgive us unless we forgive others who trespass against us (Matthew 6:14–15).

Why is it so important to God that we forgive others? It seems sometimes that God is being overly demanding. What's the big deal? Paul explains what the big deal is in his second letter to the Corinthian church. He writes, "...what I have forgiven—if there was anything to forgive—I have forgiven in the sight of Christ for your sake, in order that Satan might not outwit us. For we are not unaware of his schemes"(2 Corinthians 2:11-12). In other words, when we forgive one another, rather than passing judgment, we are avoiding one of Satan's schemes which is creating division in our ranks. *Divide and conquer* is one of Satan's top strategies against Christians. Thankfully, Satan is not our commander-in-chief. Jesus is. He said, "Every kingdom divided against itself will be ruined, and every city or household divided against itself will not stand" (Matthew 12:25). Forgiveness is imperative to maintain unity within the church.

So instead of judging, we choose mercy. Remember the story in John 8 about the woman who was caught in the very act of adultery? The scribes and Pharisees brought her to Jesus asking

> **Divide and conquer is one of Satan's top strategies against Christians.**

if he thought she should be stoned, the way Moses commanded in the law (Deuteronomy 22:24). Did Jesus judge her harshly, the way she deserved? No, he saved the woman's life with one simple statement, "He that is without sin among you, let him first cast a stone at her" (John 8:7). All of her accusers left without throwing a single stone. Nobody argued with Jesus. No one disputed the justice of his response, "for all have sinned and fall short of the glory of God" (Romans 3:23).

Jesus was living out what he had preached to his disciples when he said: "Be merciful, just as your Father is merciful. Do not judge, and you will not be judged. Do not condemn, and you will not be condemned. Forgive, and you will be forgiven" (Luke 6:36-37). The commands are clear. First, we are to be merciful just as our Father is merciful. Secondly, we are not to judge unless we want to be judged ourselves.

Does this mean that the perpetrator will go unpunished? No, it doesn't. David, a "man after God's own heart" (1 Samuel 13:14, Acts 13:22) knew whose job it was to judge and avenge. Remember the story where King Saul went into a cave to relieve himself and David cut off the corner of his robe? King Saul went back to his troops. When he was a distance away, David called after him and revealed what he had done.

Then he said, "May the Lord judge between you and me. And may the Lord avenge the wrongs you have done to me, but my hand will not touch you" (I Samuel 24:12). David left both the judging and the avenging to God.

In the New Testament, Paul reiterates the same concept in his letter to the Romans when he said, "Do not take revenge, my dear friends, but leave room for God's wrath, for it is written: 'It is mine to avenge; I will repay,' says the Lord" (Romans 12:19). God will take care of any avenging that needs to happen.

Another good reason to show mercy goes back to our initial lesson about the parable of The Unforgiving Servant. Do you remember why the king got so mad at him? He had gotten into debt and owed a whole bunch of money, but after he was forgiven, the Unforgiving Servant then went out and judged someone else for committing the exact same offense on a much smaller scale. Paul addressed this same issue in his letter to the Romans. He wrote:

> So when you, a mere human being, pass judgment on them and yet do the same things, do you think you will escape God's judgment? Or do you show contempt for the riches of his kindness, forbearance and patience, not realizing that God's kindness is intended to lead you to repentance?
>
> —ROMANS 2:3-4

Remember why we don't judge? Because we don't want to be judged ourselves. God does not take kindly when we show contempt for his immeasurable kindness, forbearance and patience towards us. God's goal when he shows us mercy is to lead us to repentance. He also wants us to pass that mercy on to others.

Before he closes out his letter to the Romans, Paul revisits the concept of not judging again in chapter 14 where he writes:

> You, then, why do you judge your brother or sister? Or why do you treat them with contempt? For we will all stand before God's judgment seat. It is written:
>
> "'As surely as I live,' says the Lord, 'every knee will bow before me; every tongue will acknowledge God.'"[17]
>
> So then, each of us will give an account of ourselves to God.
>
> — ROMANS 14:10-12

It is so easy to forget as we judge others, that we too must give account to God for our actions—and he knows the truth about everything. There is not a chance that you can pull one over on God and fool him.

In line with the knowledge that we have to give account to God, James reminds us to, "Speak and act as those who are going to be judged by the law that gives freedom, because judgment without mercy will be shown to anyone who has not been merciful. Mercy triumphs over judgment" (James 2:12-13). James starts out by telling us to speak and act as people who are going to be judged by the "law that gives freedom." It seems like a contradiction to talk about a "law that gives freedom," but that is exactly what God's law does. His law is the opposite of many human laws because his ways are not our ways. He thinks differently than we do (Isaiah 55:8). God knows that when we forgive and show mercy instead of judging we will have freedom. We won't be carrying around heavy burdens of anger and resentment. Obeying God's laws is what gives us freedom. In God's kingdom we will reap what we sow (Galatians 6:7) and "mercy triumphs over judgment" (James 2:13).

Another trap that we sometimes fall into is acknowledging God's ways, but using the excuse that "I'm just not there yet." We want to hold onto and savor our grudge a little bit longer. We like the feeling of control and superiority that we feel when we are holding something against someone we don't particularly like (or maybe we even hate them) because of how they have acted towards us. If that is you, I would like to give you a word of encouragement and a word of caution.

> **You are just one breathe away from eternity at all times.**

First, the word of encouragement. God will never ask you to do something without enabling you to obey. It may not be easy. It may, in fact, be rather painful to stop judging and forgive. But if you will sincerely ask God to help you and pick up your cross, he will help you carry it.

Now for the word of caution. None of us know how much time we or anyone else has left. In James 5:9 we read, "Don't grumble against one another, brothers and sisters, or you will be judged. The Judge is standing at the door!" As you nurse your grudge and grumble against others, keep in mind that the only moment you are promised is now. You are just one breathe away from eternity at all times. The Golden Rule is a wonderful standard. "Do to others as you would have others do to you" (Matthew 7:12). Choose mercy.

Forgiveness Story

Halfway Down the Aisle

I was visiting my old church that Sunday—the one that I grew up in. To put things in context, I have to tell you that this was the type of church that told you what to wear, what to do in your free time, even what to eat sometimes. There were definitely some control issues there.

After a decade of living away from it all, I had moved back close to home. I wasn't entirely sure about returning to my childhood church, but I felt that despite their at times misguided attempts to do what was right, they did love God. Yes, they might overstep their bounds sometimes, but I was grown up and married now and much more independent. Besides, I still had family members who attended there, which swayed my choice in that direction.

The sermon that morning was on forgiveness. The message really impacted me. As the service drew to a close, I felt that inner nudging. God was trying to tell me something.

Go tell Beth that you're sorry for holding a grudge against her and her family. Ask her for forgiveness.

Are you kidding me? She should be apologizing for all the things that she and her pastor husband did to my family! They were judgmental and harsh, not toward me in particular that much, but against my family—yes.

You need to go and tell her that you are sorry for holding unforgiveness toward her and her family.

But God, it's been over 10 years now. I really don't have a personal vendetta against her or anything. I mean, it was her husband who was more to blame... and it was my family that they wronged more than me personally.

Go.

There was no room left for argument. The service ended and I knew what I had to do, even though I felt like a fool doing it.

Did she have to sit in the front row? It's been over a decade! She's not even going to know what I'm talking about and I'm not even sure that I can explain it myself if she asks.

I went. Dragging my feet in dread. When I got halfway up the aisle, I looked up and caught Beth's eye. She was looking straight at me and then headed my way. We met in the middle with a big hug—something we had never done before. The last time I had really interacted with her, I had been 18, and she was the mother of one of my classmates.

I told her that I was sorry and she didn't even ask why. She said that she was sorry too—for everything. It was obvious that God had also spoken to her during the service. We both blubbered and cried and laughed—and felt relieved.

You know, I obeyed. I went when God told me to, even though I felt stupid and didn't understand why. But he did. The result of my obedience was that God took away any and all bitterness I had toward *the whole leadership* of that church. I have always felt that that day was the day that God gave me the gift of forgiveness.

What do I mean by the "gift of forgiveness?" It's hard to explain, but forgiveness became easier after that. I still have to nail my flesh to the cross sometimes. I still have to choose to love, bless and do good—but God enables me to forgive more readily.

It's like when I walked down that aisle, bitterness lost its hold on me. It still talks to me and tries to influence me, but its hold on my life was broken. The shackles are off now. I thank God every day that I obeyed that Sunday, because he met me—halfway down the aisle.

Halfway Down the Aisle

After reading **Halfway Down the Aisle,** answer the following questions thoughtfully:

1. Do you have any judgmental feeling or feelings of anger toward someone that you feel are justified?

2. Have you ever considered that even though the other person offended you, God will still hold you accountable for your feelings towards them?

3. How did God work in this story when the protagonist obeyed what God was telling them to do?

4. Has there been a time in your life when you obeyed God and it caused a breakthrough for you in an area that you had been struggling in? If so, what happened?

5. What is the significance of the title of this story? Why does God sometimes require us to take the first steps towards freedom before he meets us?

What does the Bible have to say?

Let's see what scripture has to say about being angry and judging others versus forgiving, being humble, showing mercy, and trusting God to take care of our grievances.

Matthew 7:1-2
Do not judge, or you too will be judged. For in the same way you judge others, you will be judged, and with the measure you use, it will be measured to you.

1. Is "do not" a command or a suggestion? What are the consequences for disobeying God?

2. What measure does God use in judging us?

Matthew 5:22a
But I tell you that anyone who is angry with a brother or sister will be subject to judgment.

1. What does being angry with a brother or sister get us? Is that a price you want to pay?

Micah 6:8
He has shown you, O mortal, what is good. And what does the Lord require of you? To act justly and to love mercy and to walk humbly with your God.

1. What is the difference between a request and a requirement?

2. Can we "love mercy" and "walk humbly" with God while being judgmental and angry?

PRAYER

Father God, thank you that when you call me to obey, you always give me the strength that I need to carry out whatever you are asking me to do. Today I pray that you would help me recognize when I am being judgmental towards others while ignoring my own bad attitudes and disobedience towards you. Thank you for giving me a humble heart that is full of grace, mercy and forgiveness towards others. Lord, you have freely forgiven me for so much! Help me to extend your heart towards others and forgive them freely too. I confess any anger and any judgmental attitudes that I have harbored and ask that you remove them and set me free from the shackles that they have placed on me. Thank you for your forgiveness in my life. I ask these things in the name of your precious Son, Jesus. Amen.

Memory Verse:

Choose one of the previous passages that you would like to learn and make a part of your spiritual arsenal. Copy it down using your preferred Bible translation and memorize it.

_____

_____

_____

_____

_____

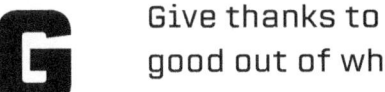

Give thanks to God that he will bring good out of what happened.

Chapter 5

Who Do You Trust?

This chapter marks the middle of our forgiveness journey. We have seen that we don't really have a right to judge others because we often mess up ourselves. We've discussed the need to release all of our offenses to God. As Christians we need to put off our "former way of life" and "be made new in the attitude of our minds" (Ephesians 4:22-23). We should not be the same people that we were before we gave our lives over to Christ. We also know that we need to repent for being judgmental and angry, since we are disobeying God's commands when we do those things. God wants us to show mercy.

Now we are ready to focus on what is often at the root of our anger towards God and others—a lack of trust that God is in absolute control of our lives and working for our good. Many of us are familiar with Romans 8:28, which tells us that "in all things God works for the good of those who love him, who have been called according to his purpose." However, when it comes down to trusting that God is working everything for good in our lives when things are going contrary to our plans—we're not really convinced.

The following is a story from the Bible that you are probably very familiar with. It's told in a way that will hopefully help you see it, and your relationship with God, in a new light.[18]

God Has a Plan

Sitting in his palace courtyard at the end of a long day, Joe absentmindedly listened to the hustle and bustle of the household around him. He did that a lot recently, since his father's death. Just last week, he and his brothers had returned from the long trek to Canaan to bury his father in the family burial plot. A servant approached with a message. His brothers were hoping for an audience with him.

He read the message they had sent, then read it again, and wept. After all these years they still didn't understand. His brothers were so afraid of revenge and retaliation that they had made up some message from their deceased father saying that he wanted Joe to forgive them for how badly they had treated him. He knew that his father had left no such instructions because his father knew he had forgiven his brothers long ago. Joe and his father understood why things had happened the way they had. They both knew who was in control of their lives. It hadn't been an easy lesson to learn. He remembered one day in particular like it was yesterday.

Who Do You Trust?

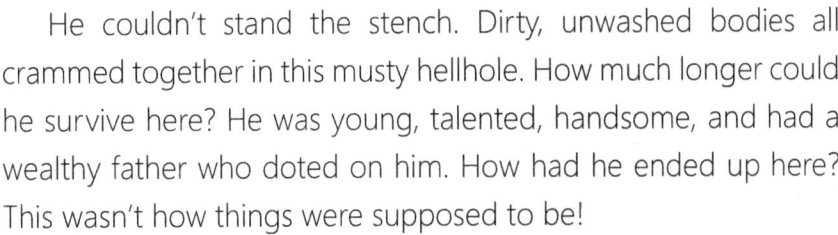

He couldn't stand the stench. Dirty, unwashed bodies all crammed together in this musty hellhole. How much longer could he survive here? He was young, talented, handsome, and had a wealthy father who doted on him. How had he ended up here? This wasn't how things were supposed to be!

How many times had he heard his father tell of the special covenant that God—the Creator of the universe—had made with his family. They were special. The Most High God had chosen them and was going to turn them into a mighty nation. He had even promised to give them the land that they were living in as an inheritance. When he was younger, he used to ask his father to repeat the stories to him over and over again. He had never doubted any of it—until now.

To be honest, back then Joe had felt that special relationship himself. He used to feel so close to God—like he could reach out and touch him almost. Those dreams he had had seemed so real. He had been so sure that God favored him and had a special plan for his life. His father seemed to concur. Although he was the second youngest of all his brothers, he had always favored him with a leadership role in the family business—something which did not exactly endear Joe to his older siblings.

But what had happened to all of that? How had he ended up here? Surely God had forsaken him. How else could he have gone from a life of sheltered privilege to this prison cell? From favored son, to slave, to prisoner. Why him? Why not one of his lying, cheating, irresponsible older brothers? He hadn't done anything to deserve any of this. Did God hate him?

Despair filled his soul as flies buzzed in the stifling heat and sweat trickled down his back. He had been here for over two years now with no end to his suffering in sight. He had thought that maybe the king's servant would appreciate the dream he had interpreted for him and pull some strings to help get him out of here, but no such luck.

He was innocent. He hadn't done anything wrong! Why was he here? It was because he was honest with his father about his brothers' behavior that his brothers had wanted to get rid of him and had sold him into slavery. (He still couldn't believe they had faked his death to his father, who had then thought that he was dead for all those years.) It was because he refused to sleep with his boss's wife when she tried to seduce him that he had ended up in prison now. Doing the right thing kept getting him in trouble.

God? Where are you? Why am I here? I'm not sure if I love you or hate you! Those dreams seemed so real. I felt so sure that your hand and your favor were upon me. What happened? What are you doing? What do you want?

It would be so much easier to go along with the crowd and do what everyone else does... Take the easy road and make the people around me happy, rather than trying to make you happy. Why do I have to be so different?

Like a whisper in his heart he had heard God reply to him that day...

I chose you. I love you! Through all of your suffering, I have never left you. It was I who caused your brothers to throw you into that dry well rather than kill you like they had planned. It was I who had them sell you into slavery. It was I who caused the slave traders who bought you to see your value and therefore not mistreat you or beat you. It was I who caused you to be sold as a slave to one of the top officials in the land so that you might learn the language of this people and the customs and manners of the ruling class. And it was I who caused you to be cast into prison, so that you might learn humility and the value of the humblest of lives. Yet even here, have I not put you in charge of the entire prison?

Your training has not been easy, but all of it has been necessary for the special plan that I have for your life. The dreams that you dreamed as a young boy were from me and will come to pass in my perfect timing. I am preparing you for that day. Meanwhile, all you need to do is have faith and keep doing your best at whatever I set before you to do. My plans for you far exceed your wildest dreams. Trust me!

Faith. It had taken all the faith Joe could muster to believe those words. To trust. To believe that the God of his fathers was working behind the scenes for his good. Yet, when he made that choice, Joe had felt the anger, hatred, and resentment toward his former owner and his brothers begin to fade away.

When Joe was finally called to the palace of Pharaoh, he was ready for the next step in his training. He *knew* who was directing his life. When his brothers had shown up nine years later, Joe was able to forgive them completely. When he saw their changed lives he could embrace them with true love.

They were here in his palace now. Waiting. He prayed that God would give him the right words to lay their fears to rest once and for all.

He walked into the audience room where they waited. His brothers threw themselves prostrate on the floor before him.

"We are your slaves!"

"No!" Joe replied. The tears still glistened in his eyes.

"You are my brothers! Why are you still so afraid? Am I God to judge you? Yes, you intended to harm me, but God intended it for good. Can't you see how many lives have been saved because of what happened? Rest easy! You were forgiven long ago. I will provide for you and for your children. You are my family. Remember, God has a plan for our lives, and his plans are always good!"

Account loosely based on parts of Genesis 37 – 50.

Forgiveness Story

If I Had Only Known...

It was around three o'clock that Friday afternoon. I was counting down the hours until the weekend started. I couldn't wait! Today had been a hectic day and I was ready for some relaxation.

I couldn't believe it had been four years since I started working here at this manufacturing plant unloading trucks in the receiving department. Back then I had been grateful to find a job with regular hours and health insurance for my family. With three growing girls at home, you never knew when something might happen that would require medical care. The pay was minimal, but with my wife's careful budgeting we were able to get by.

Thankfully, the boss had noticed my work ethic soon after I started. It wasn't long before I was moved indoors to a desk job as the cost analyst in the purchasing department. The raise had been a godsend, but since we had bought our modest home, we were still pretty much living from paycheck to paycheck.

That morning I had finished a price comparison study between the items that we were making locally and similar items being made at headquarters. Before lunch, at the meeting with the plant manager and the corporate vice-president, we had gone over my figures. My numbers were solid, and they were pleased with the results. It would be interesting to see what the next four years held in store.

The phone ringing on my desk jolted me back to the present.

The plant manager wanted to see me in his office. I supposed he had some final question about the information we had gone over that morning. Hopefully it wouldn't take too long. There were a couple of things that I wanted to finish up before five o'clock. I headed to his office. When I arrived he told me to have a seat and then closed the door. Okay... I should have known this was more than a routine figure double-check by the seriousness of his demeanor. But because I was confident in the quality of my work, I was totally caught off guard when the plant manager told me that I was being laid off. He told me to clean out my desk. I didn't need to come back to work on Monday.

In shock, I got up and returned to my desk. I kept repeating in my head what the plant manager had said, but it didn't add up. And by the way, whatever happened to giving two weeks' notice? By the time my desk was cleared out and five o'clock had rolled around, I found out that seventeen other people had also been laid off from the plant that afternoon. In a way that made me feel better because I wasn't the only one, but at the same time I knew that it would make getting another job that much harder in the small, rural town where we lived.

I felt like a total failure. There was so much that I wanted to be able to do for my family, but no matter how hard I tried I just couldn't seem to get ahead. It had been a little over a year since my wife had undergone emergency surgery for a blocked colon. Thankfully, the cancerous tumor was contained. After having to endure a colostomy bag for a year and repeated radiation treatments, my wife was told by the doctor that there were no signs of cancer. God had been so good to us! We knew that my wife's healing was a miracle from God. But there had been bills...

Was that really why I was let go? My company was self-insured and my wife's medical expenses had topped $50,000 when all was said and done. It wasn't fair! What if there were further problems and I didn't have a job? No, I *knew* God had healed her, and I wasn't going to let my thoughts go down that road.

However, during the twenty-minute drive home my thoughts went down a lot of other less-than-positive roads. Would I be able to find another job in time? Would we lose our home? Would we be able to keep our two daughters in braces? The unemployment would only last so long, and even that wouldn't keep us current on all of our bills. Our town was the kind where everything was based on who you knew—and I didn't know the right people. Hopelessness was taking over my thoughts. *God, why is this happening? Why are you doing this to us? Haven't we been through enough recently? You have to help us!* I screamed inside. There was nowhere else to turn. It seemed like my world had spun out of orbit and was hurtling rapidly into the unknown.

I felt totally defeated. So many unanswered questions were swirling around in my mind. By the time I arrived home despair was written all over my face. When my seventeen-year-old daughter opened the door she could tell that something major was wrong. She later said that she had never seen me so down before.

My daughter asked me what had happened. I choked out the story of being let go from my job. Then my daughter began to remind me of all the times in the past when God had taken care of us. We had never gone hungry. We had always had a roof over our heads and clothes on our backs. True, we might have to go without some things until I found another job, but God had not forsaken us. At first I wasn't registering what she was saying, but slowly her words of encouragement began to soak in. For the next thirty minutes she poured back into me all of the godly promises and principles I had worked so hard to instill in her and her siblings over the years. It was a humbling experience.

We had a meeting that evening to discuss the changes that we were going to have to make as a family. Everyone agreed to work together to help get us through whatever lay ahead. I would begin to look for another job come Monday. At least that was the plan.

Sunday afternoon, however, there was a knock on the front door. Theo, one of the neighbors who attended our church, was standing there. He asked if he could come in for a moment. We sat down. He told me that he had a business proposition for me. He had heard that I had been laid off. He said that he owned his own appraisal and legal abstracting company and asked if I would like to see if that was something that I would be interested in. He wouldn't be able to pay me for the first month or two while I was training with him, but he assumed that I would be getting unemployment that would help me over the hump until I was able to work independently.

That evening my wife and I prayed. We felt like this was God's provision for our family, so I called Theo up and said that yes, I would love to try working for him. He told me he would pick me up the next morning at 8:00 am. And so started my new career.

Was the work easy? No. Was it frustrating at times? Yes. Did I still worry about whether or not I would be able to support my family doing this? Yes.

I soon discovered that the appraisal part of the business was not for me, but I actually enjoyed the legal abstracting and title search work. I was good at it, too. It was like a complex logic puzzle that needed to be figured out and I loved the mental challenge.

Right about the time that I was getting ready to start working on my own, Theo told me that he was going to be moving out of the area. Would I be interested in buying his legal abstracting business from him? He set a reasonable price, but we were broke. Between just starting to get past my wife's medical bills and then subsisting off of unemployment for several months, we had no wiggle room at all.

I went to the bank and applied for a business loan putting up our home as collateral, along with our car, the business potential, etc., but their answer was no. God, however, was working on Theo's heart. When I told him that I was interested but just couldn't come up with the money, he told me that he would be willing to let me buy the business from him in monthly installments. Once again God was making a way.

My wife and I were so thankful for how God was working to provide for our family, but I won't lie and say it was easy. My first week as the business owner we didn't get a single work order. Trusting God under those circumstances took a lot of faith! However, I hung in there and prayed a lot, and sure enough the orders gradually began to come in. My wife went back to teaching to give us some financial stability until the business could support us. After several years she was able to quit—because I needed her help!

Fast forward thirty years...

This year I turn eighty—and I'm still running that legal abstracting business with my wife. Things have slowed down from our peak when we had two offices and a dozen employees, but my wife and I have kept working. Over the years, all but one of my children have worked for us. We were able to buy a nicer house and even do some traveling that would never have been possible on my former salary—or the limited retirement that I would have gotten when I was forced to quit working at sixty-five. We have been to Europe several times, as well as going on a number of international cruises. Best of all, we are still healthy and mentally alert!

I have thanked God many times over the years that I was let go that Friday afternoon. At the time, it seemed like the end of the world. I couldn't see how our family was going to make it through another crisis. But I was let go because God had something better in store for me, and my family.

So often our vision is limited to what we can see, but it's important that we trust the One who knows what lies down the road! Now I can look back and I know that getting laid off was a blessing from God. His timing was perfect and his direction was perfect. Was it an easy road to begin with? No. Pruning a tree never seems like it will help produce more fruit, but it does. When your life seems to be spiraling out of control, let go of any anger, fear, bitterness or unforgiveness that are trying to rob you of your future. Trust God to do his thing. He loves you and has great things in store for you!

If I Had Only Known...

After reading **If I Had Only Known...**, answer the following questions thoughtfully:

1. Have your life plans ever derailed unexpectedly? What happened?

2. Did you find yourself getting mad at God or at other people because of what happened? Are you still angry now?

3. What was the final outcome of your circumstances? Was it ever as bad as you had feared it would be? Did what happened to you actually end up being for your good?

4. What would your advice be for someone who finds their world spinning out of orbit? What words of encouragement could you share?

5. What will you do differently next time your life plans go awry?

What does the Bible have to say?

Often we get angry and bitter at people or circumstances that have somehow messed up our life plans—our idea of how things are supposed to be. How can surrendering our plans to God and trusting him, help us to forgive others and not hold grudges?

Proverbs 3:5-6 (NKJV)
Trust in the Lord with all your heart, and lean not on your own understanding; In all your ways acknowledge him, and he shall direct your paths.

1. Do you ever find your "own understanding" to be in conflict with what God wants to do in your life? Think of a time when God was right and you are glad that you trusted him even though it made no sense at the time.

2. Has "leaning on your own understanding," or doing things your way, ever gotten you in trouble with God or blocked his blessings in your life? Explain.

3. List two ways that you can acknowledge God in your everyday decisions.

Proverbs 19:21
Many are the plans in a person's heart, but it is the Lord's purpose that prevails.

1. What's the difference between a *plan* and a *purpose*? Do you want your *plan* for your life to win or God's *purpose* for your life to win? Are you willing to step out of the way when your plans and God's purpose collide?

Romans 8:28
And we know that in all things God works for the good of those who love him, who have been called according to his purpose.

1. Do you love God? If you do, Jesus says that you should obey him (John 14:15). Are you prepared to do that even if it doesn't make sense to you?

2. There's that word *purpose* again. Do you believe that God has a purpose for your life?

Isaiah 26:3
You will keep in perfect peace those whose minds are steadfast (unmovable)[19], because they trust in you.

1. Do you really trust God with your life? Is that trust unmovable?

PRAYER

Father God, when my life seems to be falling apart and everything seems to be going wrong and nothing is going according to my plan, help me to keep my mind stayed on you. Rather than getting angry at you or others, help me to trust in your sovereign purpose for my life. Help me to know that as I trust in you with all my heart, rather than leaning on my own understanding, that you have promised to direct my path. Thank you for your peace. Thank you that you have my life and my future in the palms of your hands. You know what lies ahead in my life and I can trust you to do what is best for me. I surrender my life to your plans. I pray these things in Jesus' name. Amen.

Memory Verse:

Choose one of the previous passages that you would like to learn and make a part of your spiritual arsenal. Copy it down using your preferred Bible translation and memorize it.

_____

_____

_____

_____

_____

F
O
R
G
I Invest in praying for the person who offended or hurt you.
V
E

Chapter 6

Forgiveness Is a Key to Answered Prayer

We have come to the fifth step in our forgiveness journey. In the last chapter we learned about thanking God that he will bring good out of whatever happened. Knowing that God has a plan for our lives and trusting him with everything that happens to us makes it easier to forgive others and to let go of offenses.

Now we're going to talk about the relationship between forgiveness and prayer. Three different times in the gospels and once in his parables, Jesus said that we have to forgive others if we want God to forgive us. It was very interesting to me that Jesus made two of the above statements about forgiveness when he was talking to his disciples about prayer. This was not accidental, as we will see. Prayer and forgiveness have a symbiotic relationship—you must pray to ask God for forgiveness and you must forgive to get your prayers answered.

The first time that Jesus links forgiveness closely with prayer is one that you probably already know. Jesus is teaching his disciples how to pray. Let's read the Lord's Prayer along with the two verses that immediately follow. It may sound different than you're used to because I have taken out two words and substituted their underlined definitions[20] (original word in parentheses). Jesus said:

> "This, then, is how you should pray:
>
> "'Our Father in heaven, hallowed be your name, your kingdom come, your will be done, on earth as it is in heaven. Give us today our daily bread. **And forgive us our debts,** <u>to the same degree</u> (as) **we also have forgiven our debtors.** And lead us not into temptation but deliver us from the evil one.'
>
> <u>Because</u> (for) **if you forgive other people when they sin against you, your heavenly Father will also forgive you. But if you do not forgive others their sins, your Father will not forgive your sins** (Emphasis mine).
>
> —MATTHEW 6:9-15

You probably already knew that the Lord's Prayer included asking God to forgive you. You may or may not have realized that it asks God to forgive us to the same extent that we forgive others. It's kind of like saying, "God, please forgive me to the same degree that I forgave my neighbor who ran over my dog last week and who I am still not talking to..." Oops! You're not going to get a whole lot of forgiveness out of that prayer, now are you?

To make his point very clear, Jesus went on to say in the two verses immediately following the Lord's Prayer, "<u>Because</u> (for) if you forgive other people when they sin against you, your heavenly Father will also forgive you. But if you do not forgive others their sins, your Father will not forgive your sins" (Matthew 6:14-15). Notice the "if." It implies that there is a condition to be met here. If you didn't forgive the neighbor who ran over your dog, then don't count on God forgiving you. That's how he works. Remember The Parable of the Unforgiving Servant in Chapter 2? This is a very important point that Jesus is trying to get across.

Now focus on the sentence that is sandwiched between the two passages about forgiveness. It says, "And lead us not into temptation but deliver us from the evil one" (Matthew 6:13). Now I don't usually go into original language meanings, but in this case I believe that doing so enriches the text. The following excerpts concerning this verse are gleaned from *Clark's Commentary on the Bible* from *Biblehub.com*:[21]

> **And lead us not into temptation** - That is, bring us not into sore trial. Πειρασμον, which may be here rendered sore trial, comes from πειρω, to pierce through, as with a spear... The word not only implies violent assaults from Satan, but also sorely afflictive circumstances, none of which we have, as yet, grace or fortitude sufficient to bear... **But deliver us from evil**... Deliver us – Ρυσαι ημας – a very expressive word – break our chains, and loose our bands – snatch, pluck us from the evil, and its calamitous issue... Απο του πονηρου, from the wicked one. Satan is expressly called ο πονηρος, the wicked one. (Emphasis mine)

Now let's reread the original text substituting in the new (underlined) meanings we have learned.

> This, then, is how you should pray:
>
> Our Father in heaven, hallowed be your name, your kingdom come, your will be done, on earth as it is in heaven. Give us today our daily bread. And forgive us our debts, <u>to the same degree</u> (as) we also have forgiven our debtors. <u>Don't bring us into sore trials which we cannot bear, but snatch us from the wicked one</u>. (end prayer)
>
> <u>Because</u> (for) if you forgive other people when they sin against you, your heavenly Father will also forgive you. But if you do not forgive others their sins, your Father will not forgive your sins.
>
> —MATTHEW 6:10-15 (paraphrased)

The big question now is *why is that sentence about "Don't bring us into sore trials that we cannot bear, but snatch us from the wicked one" thrown between two passages on forgiveness?* Is it even related? Well, the sentence right after it begins with "because" which means they are related—and even interdependent.

A look at 2 Corinthians 2:10-11 may help clarify what Jesus is trying to tell us. Paul wrote, "Anyone you forgive, I also forgive. And what I have forgiven—if there was anything to forgive—I have forgiven in the sight of Christ for your sake, in order that Satan might not outwit us. For we are not unaware of his schemes." Now we know that Satan is a liar (John 8:44b). What is his plot?

What is he scheming against us? Satan knows that Jesus' death on the Cross purchased our complete forgiveness. But he also knows that Jesus told us very clearly, several times, that if we don't forgive others, GOD WILL NOT FORGIVE US. When Satan lies to us to get us to hold grudges and not forgive others, he is trying to entrap us. When we listen to him, we are allowing him to put chains on us and lay claim to us. Are any of your grudges or complaints against others worth losing your relationship with God over? Remember, one of Satan's best strategies is to divide and thus conquer us.

When we pray the Lord's Prayer, we are asking our heavenly Father to forgive us to the same degree that we forgive others so that we won't be brought into sore trials that we cannot bear which put us under Satan's control! Why? Because if we don't forgive others, God won't forgive us. This is not an optional item on the checklist. This is not a trivial matter. Forgiving others is vital to our walk with God. It may be a matter of spiritual life and death. Don't fall for Satan's schemes!

Now let's look at another passage where Jesus links forgiveness with prayer. In Mark 11:24, Jesus is in Jerusalem for the final Passover with his disciples before the Crucifixion. In this passage he is talking to his disciples about the fig tree that had withered and died after he had cursed it the day before. His lesson to his disciples is about prayer, faith, and forgiveness. Jesus said,

> Therefore I say to you, whatever things you ask when you pray, believe that you receive them, and you will have them. "And whenever you stand praying, if you have anything against anyone, forgive him, that your

> Father in heaven may also forgive you your trespasses. But if you do not forgive, neither will your Father in heaven forgive your trespasses."
>
> —MARK 11:24-26 NKJV

The first part is so encouraging to read. "...Whatever things you ask when you pray, believe that you receive them, and you will have them" (Mark 11:24). But then Jesus adds, "And whenever you stand praying, if you have anything against anyone, forgive him, that your Father in heaven may also forgive you your trespasses" (Mark 11:25). So, *whenever* we pray, or anytime we pray, we should also forgive *anything* we have against *anyone*. It doesn't say, "*sometimes* when you pray..." nor does it say to forgive *some things* that you have against *some people*. It says, "whenever you stand praying, if you have anything against anyone, forgive him..." (Mark 11:25, emphasis mine). There are no exceptions listed here. Why? Just like we read after the Lord's Prayer, because if we don't forgive others, God will not forgive us.

Now, many of us might be saying, *What? I don't get the connection here. What does forgiveness have to do with prayer?* But any good Jewish person knew that if God didn't forgive them, he wouldn't hear them either. Let's take a look at a couple of Old Testament scriptures that Jesus' disciples would have probably been familiar with:

> If I had cherished sin in my heart, the Lord would not have listened...
>
> —PSALM 66:18

> The Lord is far from the wicked, but he hears the prayer of the righteous.
>
> —PROVERBS 15:29

> Surely the arm of the Lord is not too short to save, nor his ear too dull to hear. But your iniquities have separated you from your God; your sins have hidden his face from you, so that he will not hear.
>
> —ISAIAH 59:1-2

We see in these scriptures that sin, wickedness and iniquities will all keep God from hearing us.

Think of prayer as being dependent on a spiritual WiFi connection to God. In my house, the wireless modem is downstairs and my bedroom is upstairs at the other end of the house. Usually this is not a problem, but sometimes I'm lying in bed trying to access the internet and there is just plain no connection. I've learned that the first thing I need to do is check to see if the door to my bedroom is open, because a closed door is a guaranteed loss of connection.

Sin is a closed-door event. It keeps God from hearing us. How do we get rid of sin? We ask God to forgive us, right? But we just read in Mark that if we don't forgive others, God will not forgive us. So, to get rid of the closed door that keeps God from hearing us, we have to start by forgiving others. See, when we forgive others, God is free to forgive us all of the sins, the wickedness and the iniquities that are keeping him from hearing us. This opens wide the door of communication between us and God. This is powerful stuff! So many people stop praying because they say that God doesn't answer their prayers. Maybe, he just can't hear us sometimes because of choices that we have made.

Although God is not your personal genie and will not answer all of anyone's prayers on demand, he does delight in answering his children that are in right standing with him. Let's read a few scriptures that talk about God hearing prayer.

> We know that God does not listen to sinners. He listens to the godly person who does his will.
>
> —JOHN 9:31

> If you remain in me and my words remain in you, ask whatever you wish, and it will be done for you.
>
> —JOHN 15:7

> Dear friends, if our hearts do not condemn us, we have confidence before God and receive from him anything we ask, because we keep his commands and do what pleases him.
>
> —I JOHN 3:21-22

The first of these three scriptures starts out with "We *know* that God does not listen to sinners." That was common knowledge to Jesus' disciples. The next two promises, however, contain "if." Both verses talk about listening to and obeying either Jesus' words or God's commandments—which include the importance of forgiving others when we approach God in prayer. Forgiving *anyone, anything, whenever* we pray will keep open the door of communication with our heavenly Father. It will also keep our heart from condemning us so that we have confidence before God when we pray.

We are all sinners by nature (Ecclesiastes 7:20, Romans 3:10-12). It's obvious that we ALL need forgiveness. So what do we have to do if we want God to forgive us? We have to forgive others. His forgiveness, bought through the blood of Jesus, makes us righteous and opens up the door so that God can hear our prayers.

So now we understand that forgiving others is a vital key to getting our prayers answered. It keeps our pathways of communication open with God. However, not only is forgiveness vital to getting our prayers answered, but the opposite is also true. Prayer is vital to receiving forgiveness. See, after we forgive others, we still need God to forgive us. How do we communicate with God? Through prayer! We read in 2 Chronicles 7:14, "if my people, who are called by my name, will humble themselves and pray and seek my face and turn from their wicked ways, then I will hear from heaven, and I will forgive their sin and will heal their land."

> **Forgiving *anyone*, *anything*, whenever we pray will keep open the door of communication with our heavenly Father.**

Step one: forgive others.

Step two: ask God to forgive you.

Step three: see God move in your life.

It's that easy! Forgiving others and asking God to forgive us whenever we pray is a key that opens up the doorway to God hearing and answering our prayers.

Forgiveness Story

It Will Change Your Life

There was no way I was going to pray for that woman! I didn't care what my mom said. Praying for her would fix absolutely nothing. I was so mad I could spit nails! She was such a hypocrite, and I hated hypocrites! How could she write me up when she did the same thing herself almost every day? It was wrong on so many levels...

My seventeen-year-old mind was steaming! I would almost say that I hated her. Trina. My supervisor at the soup kitchen. She called herself a Christian, but all she did was find fault. Nothing I did was ever good enough, fast enough or done right. Then there was me. I was the type of person who *hated* getting in trouble. I was a perfectionist and a rule follower. Her nitpicky fault-finding was about to send me over the edge.

She didn't even seem to appreciate that she was getting all this work for *free*. Why was I putting up with all of the abuse that she piled on me? Because I had signed up for it, and in my family you didn't just quit because things were harder than you expected.

Up until today I had just worked harder and tried to show Trina that I was giving her my best efforts. But today she crossed the line. She wrote me up and I got called into the director's office. Why? I had spilled something all over my one pair of tennis shoes the day before. So, I had worn sandals to work while my tennis shoes were getting washed. I knew that I was supposed to wear closed-toed shoes in the kitchen, and I had—every day except for today. The director had a meeting with me and put me on warning saying it was "a safety issue." What had me steaming was that Trina had worn sandals in the kitchen most of the summer, and *she* was the one who wrote me up!

When I pointed that little detail out to the director, she was unimpressed. Probably because the other reason that I had been written up was for being disrespectful. Yes, I had challenged Trina on the fact that she didn't wear the right shoes most of the time herself. I was upset that my supervisor was getting away with something that she was writing me up for. Did I mention that I *hated* getting in trouble?

I was told that the problem was not that I had pointed out Trina's shoe problem, but rather *how* I had pointed it out. I should have told her that I was *concerned for her safety* and that I *didn't want her to get hurt*. I should have said that I was *worried that a knife might fall and cause her injury* (I wished!). The injustice and hypocrisy of it all was too much for me. And now my mother was taking their side and even telling me that I should pray for Trina. She was crazy!

My mom told me to try praying for Trina for a couple of weeks and see what happened. I felt that I had little choice because I still had over a month before the summer would be over. I was stuck with Trina for another five weeks at least.

So, I tried it. Whenever I started getting mad at Trina—which initially was every time I saw her—I prayed for her. I prayed that God would bless her, watch over her, and show her his love. At first I spit the words out and didn't mean them at all. I just wanted to prove to my mother that her stupid idea wouldn't work. But, it didn't take long before my attitude started to change. It is very hard to pray blessing on someone and stay mad at them. Before long my prayers were sincere and heartfelt. Then, amazingly, Trina started to be nice. She stopped picking on me and started complimenting my work. I couldn't believe it!

By the end of the summer I wanted to stay on at the soup kitchen. Trina loved me and offered to write me a letter of recommendation. I would leave there with fond memories and a new friend and advocate.

By praying for Trina, God turned my bitterness, resentment and anger into forgiveness and love. If God can do that for me, he can do it for you too! Jesus said "Bless them that curse you, and pray for them which despitefully use you" (Luke 6:28). Try it. It will change your life.

It Will Change Your Life

After reading *It Will Change Your Life*, answer the following questions thoughtfully:

1. Have you ever had a run-in with someone who would find fault with you no matter what you did or how hard you tried? How did that make you feel?

2. Have you forgiven that person, or does the thought of them still give you a *ping* of anger or resentment? Elaborate.

3. Does it matter to God whether or not we get along with people, or is it just a fact that there will be people that we don't get along with and that's okay?

4. Have you ever prayed for someone that you were truly angry with? How long did you pray for them? What happened?

5. In the end, do you think that Trina changed or that the author changed? Why did they change in your opinion? Explain your answer.

What does the Bible have to say?

Let's see what scripture has to say about living in harmony with others and what our responsibility is in the matter.

Ephesians 4:2-3
Be completely humble and gentle; be patient, bearing with one another in love. Make every effort to keep the unity of the Spirit through the bond of peace.

1. Is it possible to be proud, antagonistic, and impatient and still live in unity with others? Why or why not?

2. What do you think Paul means when he talks about "bearing with one another in love?"

3. Jesus is called the "Prince of Peace." What do you think the "bond of peace" is that Paul says will help us "to keep the unity of the Spirit?"

Romans 12:18
If it is possible, as far as it depends on you, live at peace with everyone.

1. Romans 12 is considered to be one of the gold standards for Christian living. Why do you think Paul begins this verse with "If it be possible, as far as it depends on you...?"

2. Are there times when it might be best to walk away from a person or situation? Explain. Can you come up with a biblical basis for your answer?

Philippians 2:1-2

Therefore if you have any encouragement from being united with Christ, if any comfort from his love, if any common sharing in the Spirit, if any tenderness and compassion, then make my joy complete by being like-minded, having the same love, being one in spirit and of one mind.

1. Paul gives us an "if/then" challenge here. What is it?

2. Why should we accept his challenge?

Forgiveness Is a Key to Answered Prayer

PRAYER

Father God, I thank you that you sent your Son Jesus to live among us as the Prince of Peace. Today I ask that your peace would fill my heart. Replace any anger, hurt or resentment that I am feeling towards _____ with your love. Help me to see them through your eyes and with your heart. Lord, I pray that you would bless _____ today. Help them to feel your love and your presence in their life. You alone know the burden that they are carrying. I pray that you would lift their burdens off their shoulders and help them see your hand at work in their circumstances. Fill their heart with your peace and a calm assurance that they are not alone in the middle of their trials. May your joy be their strength. I ask these things in Jesus' name, Amen.

Memory Verse:

Choose one of the previous passages that you would like to learn and make a part of your spiritual arsenal. Copy it down using your preferred Bible translation and memorize it.

_____

_____

_____

_____

_____

View the other person through God's eyes. He loves them!

Chapter 7

It's All About Love

We are ready to take the sixth step in our forgiveness journey. In the last chapter we learned about how important forgiveness is to our communication with God. We were reminded that if we don't forgive others, God will not forgive us. We also learned how much we need that forgiveness if we want God to answer our prayers. Forgiveness keeps our lines of communication with God open, which is vital to maintaining a relationship with him.

And now we are finally going to focus on love. The good stuff, right? Everyone loves love, or so we think. There is probably not another word in the English language that is as misrepresented as the word *love*. In this chapter we are going to learn what the Bible says about love. God's love is an action—not a feeling. It is focused on others—not on self. The love God calls us to is not optional. It is a commandment that we must obey if we want to follow him.

Now you may think of commandments as Old Testament, nitpicky rules that the Israelites had to follow before Jesus came and taught about grace. But did you know that Jesus gave his disciples (that would be us) specific commandments as well? He also ratified some of the Old Testament laws. Let's take a look at a story in Matthew where a Pharisee, who was an expert in Jewish law, wanted to know what the greatest commandment was. He asked Jesus,

> "Teacher, which is the greatest commandment in the Law?"
>
> Jesus replied: "'Love the Lord your God with all your heart and with all your soul and with all your mind.' This is the first and greatest commandment. And the second is like it: 'Love your neighbor as yourself.' All the Law and the Prophets hang on these two commandments."
>
> —MATTHEW 22:36-40

Jesus said that the greatest commandment is to love God, and the second greatest commandment is to love our neighbors, or brothers, as we love ourselves. The top two commandments are both about love! Jesus also said that *all* the Law and the Prophets (all the Old Testament word of God that was not historical record) hang on these two commandments. Basically, these two commandments sum up what is truly important to God. Why is love so important? Because "God *is* love" (1 John 4:8b). Think about that for a minute... That puts a whole new spin on things, doesn't it?

It is fascinating to see how intertwined loving others and

loving God are, and how closely they are tied to obedience to God. They seem to be so interwoven at times that it is difficult to see where one ends and the other begins. For example, in 1 John 5:2-3 we read: "This is how we know that we love the children of God: by loving God and carrying out his commands. In fact, this is love for God: to keep his commands. And his commands are not burdensome..." We know that we love God's children, if we love God and keep his commandments—because his commandments say to love his children and to love him! It is impossible to truly do *any* of the three without doing *all* three.

In 2 John 1:5-6 we see the same idea about walking in God's commandments and loving one another reiterated. "... I am not writing you a new command but one we have had from the beginning. I ask that we love one another. And this is love: that we walk in obedience to his commands. As you have heard from the beginning, his command is that you walk in love." Loving God, loving one another and keeping his commandments are all synonymous—and vital to our salvation. So, to sum things up, if we love God, we will keep his commandments and his top two commandments are to love him and to love his children. With that in mind, we should probably find out how the Bible defines love.

The most comprehensive definition of love in the Bible is the one given by Paul in 1 Corinthians 13, but I want to go back to the previous chapter to put chapter 13 in context. In chapter 12, Paul starts out talking about spiritual gifts. He then proceeds to say that as Christians we are all members of one body—the Body of Christ. (It is important for us to remember that we are all members of one body—we are intrinsically connected to one another in Christ). Each member of this body is vitally important and each has different giftings.

Now, let's look at the last verse in chapter 12: "Now eagerly desire the greater gifts. And yet I will show you the most excellent way" (1 Corinthians 12:31). Paul tells us to eagerly desire the "greater" gifts of the Spirit. But those are not *the* most excellent way. *The* most excellent way, we find out in chapter 13, is the way of love. All of our other spiritual gifts such as tongues, prophecy, knowledge, and faith, mean nothing without love. They will all pass away. Only love will endure (1 Corinthians 13:8-10). Paul goes on to say that any sacrifices we make or works we do for God, mean nothing if not done in love (1 Corinthians 13:1-3).

So, what are the main characteristics of this love that is so crucial to our walk with God? Is it a warm fuzzy feeling that we feel? Is it all about us? No! God's love is quite the opposite of what we generally define as love. In 1 Corinthians 13:4 (NKJV) Paul says that "love suffers long and is kind". Do you have any idea how hard that can be? Have you ever suffered long? Like a long time—and still been kind? That is not how most humans react. But it is love. Just for fun, let's read the rest of verse 4 and several verses that follow it in the New King James Version. It's more descriptive. I am going to include some personal commentary in parentheses to explain or personalize the text. As we read, pay attention to the fact that love is not about us, but about others—and it is definitely not easy to live out in our everyday relationships. Read with me.

- "Love suffers long and is kind"
- "love does not envy" (or want what someone else has)
- "love does not parade itself, is not puffed up" (or full of itself)
- "does not behave rudely"
- "does not seek its own" (doesn't try to get its own way)
- "is not provoked" (doesn't react, get riled)
- "thinks no evil" (always gives the benefit of the doubt)
- "does not rejoice in iniquity" (isn't happy about bad things)
- "but rejoices in the truth"
- "bears all things" (puts up with a lot of junk!)
- "believes all things" (chooses to trust—God and others)
- "hopes all things" (always believes the best is possible)
- "endures all things" (keeps on bearing with things for a long time)

—1 CORINTHIANS 13: 4-7 NKJV

Did you notice that Paul's definition of love starts with suffering and ends with enduring? Love is putting another person's needs above your own without regard to fairness or payback. In fact, love is about dying to your own feelings and wants and desires and thinking about others instead.

Isn't that what God did for us? John 3:16 says, "For God so loved the world that he gave his one and only Son, that whoever believes in him shall not perish but have eternal life." Most of us know and can quote that verse, but have you ever read 1 John 3:16 and applied it to your life? It says, "This is how we know what love is: Jesus Christ laid down his life for us. *And we ought to lay down our lives for our brothers and sisters*" (Emphasis mine).

Now it's personal! It was all fine when God wanted to show his love for us by sacrificing his Son for us. We are so thankful that Jesus chose to lay down his life for us... But is he expecting us to lay down our lives for the screw-ups we go to church with? (Nothing personal; I'm one of those screw-ups too.) He is! Remember that the Cross is where love and forgiveness intersect.

1 John 3:16 is saying we must love/forgive our Christian brothers just as Jesus loved/forgave us—even if it costs us as much as it cost Him. But wait a minute! John was just repeating what Jesus had personally told him and the other disciples the night before his crucifixion. After the Last Supper, after Judas had left to betray him, Jesus shared his final thoughts with his disciples. After he told them that his time was short, the first thing he said to them was, "A new command I give you: Love one another. As I have loved you, so you must love one another. By this everyone will know that you are my disciples, if you love one another" (John 13:34-35). Wow! Did you catch that? Everyone will know that we are Jesus' disciples by our love. (Selah. Stop and think about that for a while). We have to love each other the way that Jesus loves us! He didn't go there, did he? He did.

A little later the same night Jesus said, "Greater love has no one than this: to lay down one's life for one's friends" (John 15:13). Then in the very next verse he says, "You are my friends if you do what I command" (John 15:14). He goes on a few verses later to say, "This is my command: Love each other" (John 15:17). He repeated the new commandment that He had given them a little earlier. Like a good teacher, he repeated what was important so that his disciples would remember it. *Love each other! Lay down your lives for each other!* That's what makes us friends of Jesus.

Are you his friend? Are you obeying his commandments? All of them?

Okay, so maybe you are getting the love stuff, but what role does forgiveness play in all of this? Peter said, "Above all, love each other deeply, because love covers over a multitude of sins" (1 Peter 4:8). Which means that love will forgive a multitude of sins. If you're not forgiving, it's because you're not loving. It is possible that Peter was repeating something he had learned and taken to heart from King Solomon in Proverbs 10:12, where he wrote, "Hatred stirs up conflict, but love covers over *all* wrongs" (Emphasis mine). This is why true love and forgiveness have to walk hand in hand. We have to love to forgive and forgive to love. It is really impossible to do one without doing the other for any length of time.

Now let's look at the opposite side of the coin. What happens when we hate our brother, rather than loving and forgiving him? In his first letter John wrote:

> Anyone who claims to be in the light but hates a brother or sister is still in the darkness. Anyone who loves their brother and sister lives in the light, and there is nothing in them to make them stumble. But anyone who hates a brother or sister is in the darkness and walks around in the darkness. They do not know where they are going, because the darkness has blinded them.
>
> —1 JOHN 2:9-11

Loving our brother puts us in the light, and hating our brother puts us in darkness. When we are walking in the light and loving our brothers, there is nothing in us to make us stumble—the way is clear. When we hate our brothers, everything changes. We start walking in darkness. I think the line that says, "They do not know where they are going, because the darkness has blinded them" (v. 11b), is very revealing. The person that hates a brother or sister may actually think that they are still headed in the right direction. They may think that they are following Jesus still, because that is what they want to do, but in the darkness that they're in, they have turned around and are now headed in the opposite direction—away from God. They are walking in darkness. Remember, God is love and light (1 John 4:8b; 1:5).

The Bible often refers to light and darkness, but we act as though there is a misty netherworld in between where we are not quite obeying God, but still definitely NOT obeying Satan—but that is not the case, because it is impossible. In 1 John 1:5b we read, "God is light; in him there is no darkness at all." (There is no gray scale here.)

Later in 1 John 4:20 we read, "Whoever claims to love God yet hates a brother or sister is a liar. For whoever does not love their brother and sister, whom they have seen, cannot love God, whom they have not seen." If we say we love God and hate our brother, we are not only walking in darkness, but we are liars—and Satan is the father of lies (John 8:44). That is very sobering to me! I can't afford to disobey God and I can't afford to hate my brother. Both things put my eternal future at risk.

Now, sometimes you may feel (as I do at times) that it's impossible to love certain brothers or sisters in Christ. In and of ourselves, that may be true. The wonderful thing about the God we serve is that he will always equip us for whatever he asks us to do. In Paul's first letter to the Thessalonian church he wrote: "Now about your love for one another we do not need to write to you, for you yourselves have been taught by God to love each other" (1 Thessalonians 4:9). The church in Thessalonica did not need any teaching on love because God himself had taught them to love each other already. As we seek Him, God will do that for us too!

In Romans 5:5b we further discover that "...God's love has been poured out into our hearts through the Holy Spirit, who has been given to us." God puts his love in our hearts through his Holy Spirit and thus enables us to love our brothers and sisters with his love. If you're running short on love, go to the source of love and ask for a refill! It's a gift that God wants to share with you.

The Bible also says "for it is God who works in you to will and to act in order to fulfill his good purpose"(Philippians 2:13). He works in you to **want** to do what he said and to **act** on what he said. That's a promise that you can claim and stand on in your moments of weakness.

Loving God and loving your Christian brothers and sisters are the two most important commandments. However, you can't love in the long run unless you are willing to forgive—not only God and your brother, but yourself as well. If you hate your brother, you are walking in darkness. You also can't hate your brother and say you love God, because there is no darkness in him. He is light. The good news is that you don't have to produce love for your brother by yourself. The same God who requires that we love, promises to give that love to us.

Forgiveness Story

Loving the Unlovable

I was truly miserable. Every day for the past month things had just gotten worse and worse. If I could have quit, I would have, but there just weren't very many jobs available during the hours when I could work. We needed the money. I was stuck.

As a mother of four young children, the decision to go back to work had been hard enough. I loved being a mom and watching my children, but my husband and I were really struggling to make ends meet. For several months we had worked through every possible scenario for saving money and/or cutting expenses that we could think of, but the truth was that there just wasn't enough money to go around.

My going back to work, however, would create a whole different set of challenges. If we tried paying someone to watch the kids while I worked a day job, there wouldn't be much money left over from any salary that I would make, so that wasn't really an option. We were running out of ideas, when finally, my husband and I had figured out that if he worked the early shift at the factory, then he could be back midafternoon to watch the kids and I could take the late afternoon/evening shift that had opened up at our local nursing home.

I remember thinking that working at the nursing home would be perfect for me. I was a nurse at heart. The fact that I had had to quit my nursing program halfway through when I became unexpectedly pregnant with my oldest child, didn't diminish my love for taking care of people. When I first landed the job I was ecstatic. I had done all of the practical coursework for my nursing degree and this would give me an opportunity to put my training to work.

An older certified RN and I would be the only ones working the evening shift and our main duties would be getting the residents ready for bed, dispensing their various medications, and being on call if we were needed. It didn't sound too hectic, and the shift ended at midnight. I would miss out on some sleep, but we could make this work.

I thought back to that first day. I had styled my hair, polished my shoes, put on my scrubs and double-checked everything to make sure that it was up to the standards that I had been taught in nursing school. I wanted the RN that I would be working with to know that I was a professional and serious about my duties. I was eager to make a good impression. I drove to the nursing home, parked, and double-checked my lipstick and hair before stepping out of the car. This was it!

My heart was pounding as I walked to the front entrance. What would my co-worker be like? I hoped that she would like me... I walked in the door and rang the bell on the front counter. A slovenly looking woman, in a nurse's uniform, headed towards me down the hallway. Surely this wasn't the woman that I would be working with! Her hair was on her collar (something that they had taught us was a big no-no in nursing school), her shoes looked scruffy and the heels were all run down. She had several yellowish smudges on the front of her uniform – and the shift was just starting. She definitely didn't measure up to the standards I had been taught.

I smiled, hoping the dismay and disapproval I was feeling weren't showing on my face. *Hi, I'm Nina, the new aide*, I said. *It's a good thing you're here*, she growled. *There's a lot of work to do.* This wasn't turning out the way that I had expected! The conflict began right away. Rhonda unceremoniously showed me to my locker, where I put my purse and sack dinner, before launching immediately into a list of my responsibilities. There was nothing unexpected there. During my interview, the director had explained to me that I would be helping the residents get ready for bed after dinner. What I wasn't expecting was to be treated like a simpleton. My hackles were up! Little things that shouldn't have mattered irked me to no end.

In retrospect, my own attitude was probably less than stellar. At the time, however, all I could see was this frowsy, slow, older woman who was mercilessly picking on me. *Did you get water for the people across the hall? Did **everyone** get water? What about Thomas? He did? Did you remember to give backrubs? Sally Jean needs you to be extra gentle. It's important that everyone go to the bathroom. We don't want to be cleaning up accidents. Did you double check that **all** the lights were off? Are you sure?* And on and on, night after night, for a month now.

When everyone was put to bed and we were done charting, things were just plain awkward between us. How much longer would I be able to take this? I thought about my husband scrambling around trying to get the kids bathed and settled for the night. We were both stretched pretty thin right now. Better not think about that...

Since Rhonda and I weren't really talking, I randomly picked up a pamphlet that someone had left lying on the desk hoping it would help me pass the time. It talked about God and about love. I had been a Christian for a few years now, so I thought it would be interesting to read what it said. The scripture passage from Matthew 5:43-48 (KJV) which talked about "loving your enemies" and "doing good to them that hate you" triggered a memory.

I was back in my seventh-grade Sunday school class and the teacher was challenging us to take the Golden Rule and try to apply it to our lives. "...Do to others what you would have them do to you..." (Matthew 7:12). It sounded like a wonderful idea, and I could hardly wait to try it out. At the time I had taken that challenge and applied it to a girl from school who had started spreading lies about me and acting as though I were her enemy. I decided to treat her the way I wished she would treat me. I was going to see if my Sunday school teacher was right when she said that love and kindness could turn an enemy into a friend.

It hadn't been easy. At first the other girl, Julie, rebuffed me. I think she was kind of shocked and unsure of how to react when I started being nice. However, as I doggedly continued to repay her rudeness with kindness and love, our relationship began to change. It wasn't too many months before the two of us were great friends. As a result, I came to believe that the Golden Rule was a valuable principle.

Now, as I reread Jesus' words in the pamphlet about *loving my enemies* and *praying for those who despitefully used me*, I thought, *why not pray for Rhonda and do good to her?* I knew I wouldn't last much longer if things continued the way they were.

You know, as soon as I decided that I would try to win her over with love, I saw everything about Rhonda differently. God showed me that she was so nitpicky about the residents' care because she really loved them. Her uniform was not sparkly white, because medicine stains don't always come out—even with bleach. Her shoes were worn down because she worked hard and was on her feet a lot. I realized that she was probably too tired to polish them every night anymore. The more I focused on the good in Rhonda the more good I saw. God also showed me some things about my attitude that he wanted to change.

You know what else happened? As I began to show Rhonda respect and look for the good in her, her attitude towards me changed as well. As I became less belligerent, she questioned me less and trusted me more. As we got to know each other, I was surprised to find out that Rhonda was a Christian too! We had a great time talking about our faith, and she began to share some things with me that launched me into a deeper walk with Jesus. Now, when the residents were in bed and our charting was done, the best part of the evening began.

In retrospect, it is obvious that Satan had been trying to cause division, in order to steal a blessing from both Rhonda and me. But, instead, God used Rhonda to teach me a lesson that I have remembered ever since. Loving the unlovable in obedience to Jesus, is like planting a seed that will multiply blessings back into your own life.

Loving the Unlovable

After reading **Loving the Unlovable,** answer the following questions thoughtfully:

1. Have you ever been stuck working with someone that you found to be unbearable? As a Christian, how did you deal with the situation? In retrospect what, if anything, should you have done differently?

2. Has God ever told you to focus on your own attitude and actions rather than trying to change another person's? Did you? What was the result?

3. How often do you think that pride is at the root of problems that we have getting along with others?

4. Complete the following comparison:

   Love is...   Pride is...

5. If you, as a Christian, actually obeyed Christ's commandment to love your enemies, how do you think your life would change? Would your stress levels change at all? Why or why not?

What does the Bible have to say?

Let's see what scripture has to say about how we should treat one another.

1 Peter 1:22
Now that you have purified yourselves by obeying the truth so that you have sincere love for each other, love one another deeply, from the heart.

1. Do you think that you have sincere, deep, love for your brothers and sisters in Christ? Be honest...

1 Peter 2:1
Therefore, rid yourselves of all malice and all deceit, hypocrisy, envy, and slander of every kind.

1. This verse is the follow-up to the one above. If you have sincere love for your brothers and sisters in Christ, you should have also gotten rid of malice, deceit, hypocrisy, envy and slander "of every kind." Have you? Do you have "sincere love?"

1 John 3:10
This is how we know who the children of God are and who the children of the devil are: Anyone who does not do what is right is not God's child, nor is anyone who does not love their brother and sister.

1. Whose child are you if you don't love your brothers and sisters in Christ?

2. Do you agree with what John is saying here? Why or why not?

1 John 3:14-15
We know that we have passed from death to life, because we love each other. Anyone who does not love remains in death. Anyone who hates a brother or sister is a murderer, and you know that no murderer has eternal life residing in him.

1. Have you ever considered yourself to be a murderer? Are you according to these verses?

2. Do you want eternal life? If so, what must you do according to the disciple known as "John the Beloved," Jesus' best friend while he was on earth? Do you think he knew what he was talking about?

PRAYER

Father God, thank you that you sent your Son Jesus to earth to show us how to love one another. Thank you that one of the greatest symbols of your love is the Cross. You commanded me, as your follower, to take up my own cross when I decided to follow you. Help me to realize that part of what needs to be nailed to that cross is Pride, and its cousin Self, in all its forms—self-righteousness, selfishness, self-centeredness, self-pity... I pray that you would plant your heart of love in me; a heart that seeks the good of others over my own good. Help me to see my brothers and sisters through your eyes. Help me to focus on the needs of others with love and grace and humility. Please remove any traces of hatred out of my heart. I love you! I ask these things in Jesus' name. Amen.

Memory Verse:

Choose one of the previous passages that you would like to learn and make a part of your spiritual arsenal. Copy it down using your preferred Bible translation and memorize it.

_____

_____

_____

_____

FORGIVE

Erase the repetitive voice of the enemy from your thoughts by blessing the one who hurt you every time the person or situation comes to mind.

Chapter 8

You Will Reap Exactly What You Sow— Only More of It

We are now ready to take the final step in our forgiveness journey. In the last chapter we learned how important love is to our walk with God. We learned that God's love is an action, not a feeling, and that it is focused on the good of others, not on self. We learned that not only did Jesus love us enough to lay down his life for us, but that he also commands us to do the same for our brothers and sisters. The love that we need doesn't come from us, but God gives it to us through his Holy Spirit.

In this chapter our focus is going to be on sowing and reaping— aka, planting and harvesting. We are going to see what kind of seed God wants us to be cultivating and what we need to do if we want to bear fruit. We will also learn what the consequences are for not bearing good fruit. What does this have to do with forgiveness? That's what you're about to find out.

The Law of Sowing and Reaping is one of God's foundational laws of the universe. God created the seeds that we plant in our vegetable gardens, but there are also spiritual seeds that we are constantly planting in our lives. Paul wrote to the Galatians:

> Do not be deceived: God cannot be mocked. A man reaps what he sows. Whoever sows to please their flesh, from the flesh will reap destruction; whoever sows to please the Spirit, from the Spirit will reap eternal life. Let us not become weary in doing good, for at the proper time we will reap a harvest if we do not give up.
>
> —GALATIANS 6:7-9

God allows us to choose what we plant in our lives—but he makes sure that we know ahead of time that we will harvest only what we plant. Unfortunately, in my spiritual life I am not always as intentional with my choices as I should be.

When I was a young girl on the mission field, we had a vegetable garden where we grew most of our food. We also had a number of fruit trees of different kinds. In case you've never had a garden or orchard of your own, let me tell you up front that they are a lot of work! You have to clear the weeds away, fertilize the soil, plant seeds and water them. After they sprout you have to constantly weed around your plants and care for them if you want them to be healthy and bear fruit.

Looking back, I can see how our walk with God is a lot like planting and taking care of a garden. One of the first things that we need to do if we want to bear good fruit is clear some ground from weeds so that we have a place where our new seeds can be planted and thrive. If you throw a handful of vegetable seeds into a patch of weeds, you're not going to grow much!

What are some examples of weeds that may hinder our

spiritual seeds from growing? Weeds may be tied to the internet, TV, video games, sports, work, books, hobbies, or just plain busyness. In and of themselves, these things are not evil, but anything that keeps us from spending time with God is a weed. If weeds are left alone, they will soon overtake our whole garden! We will find ourselves not having time to pray or read the Bible on a daily basis. Our relationship with God will get choked out and will be unfruitful. When Jesus explained The Parable of the Sower to his disciples, he put it this way: "Still others, like seed sown among thorns, hear the word; but the worries of this life, the deceitfulness of wealth and the desires for other things come in and choke the word, making it unfruitful" (Mark 4:18-19). These weeds are an ongoing threat to our walk with God unless we are intentional about consistently keeping our priorities straight.

In addition to clearing some space for God's seeds to grow in us, we need to fertilize and enrich the soil of our hearts. We do this by asking God to forgive our sins and to bring good out of the mistakes and hurts from our past. His healing in these areas prepares our heart for growth. Reading the Bible every day and spending time in prayer help provide the nutrients needed to grow the fruit of the Spirit in our lives.

We also need to intentionally plant God's nature in our lives. Paul said in the passage we read from Galatians 6 that we can sow to the flesh—and reap destruction—or we can sow to the Spirit— and reap eternal life. Don't believe anyone who tries to sell you "genetically modified" spiritual seed, promising that you can sow to the flesh and reap life. It's not true! If you take the truth and mix it with a little bit of deception, by definition it is no longer truth. God's Word is our standard for truth. There are only two options: death or life. You will harvest what you plant—and you will always harvest more than you planted!

Forgiveness is a seed that I have had to intentionally plant in my life. It does not come naturally to my selfish, self-centered nature. If left alone, my life would probably grow a bumper crop of resentment, bitterness, and even hatred at times. However, those things are all weeds. They are ugly and steal life from the things that my Father, God, wants growing in my life.

Cultivating forgiveness in my life has been an ongoing process. There are many weeds that try to come in and crowd forgiveness out of my heart. If I don't stay constant in my quiet time with God, the soil of my heart gets hard and dry and forgiveness starts to dry up by the roots. However, when I stay focused on how much God has forgiven me and I ask him to help me, I find that forgiveness flourishes.

I've also found that growing forgiveness in my life enables me to obey many of Jesus' other commandments, too. For example, in the book of Luke Jesus said,

> But love your enemies, do good to them, and lend to them without expecting to get anything back. Then your reward will be great, and you will be children of the Most High, because he is kind to the ungrateful and wicked. Be merciful, just as your Father is merciful. Do not judge, and you will not be judged. Do not condemn, and you will not be condemned. Forgive, and you will be forgiven.
>
> —LUKE 6:35-37

This passage starts out with "love your enemies, do good to them..." and ends with "...forgive, and you will be forgiven." Jesus called us to reverse what the enemy is trying to plant in our lives. His law is that we reap what we sow. If we don't want to harvest what our enemy is trying to plant in our lives, then we need to plant the opposite. Remember, we will enjoy the "fruits of our labor"—whether good or evil. When the enemy tries to plant bitterness in your life, reverse the harvest by planting forgiveness. When he tries to plant hatred in your life, reverse the harvest by planting love. If we do what Jesus commands us, he says that our reward will be great. We will be the children of the Highest—of Father God.

Did you notice that most of the do's and don'ts listed in the passage from Luke are not possible for us to do without forgiving others regularly? Can you "love your enemies" if you don't forgive them? Can you "be kind to the ungrateful and wicked" without forgiving them? Can you "be merciful" to undeserving people without having forgiveness in your heart towards them? What will keep you from judging and condemning others? Forgiveness! This is an essential seed to plant in our lives. We cannot walk in the steps of our Savior unless we forgive others as he has forgiven us.

> **If we don't want to harvest what our enemy is trying to plant in our lives, then we need to plant the opposite.**

Now we are faced with two important questions. What are some of the other seeds that we should be planting in our lives? And how do we identify the weeds that we should be removing from our lives? Depending on how long you have been a Christian, you may or may not have heard of the *fruit of the Spirit*. Paul, however, listed the acts (fruit) of the flesh before he listed the fruit of the Spirit. Let's look in Galatians 5 to read about both:

> <u>The acts of the flesh</u> are obvious: sexual immorality, impurity and debauchery; idolatry and witchcraft; **hatred, discord**, jealousy, **fits of rage**, selfish ambition, **dissensions, factions** and envy; drunkenness, orgies, and the like. I warn you, as I did before, that those who live like this will not inherit the kingdom of God.
>
> But <u>the fruit of the Spirit</u> is **love**, joy, peace, **forbearance, kindness**, goodness, faithfulness, gentleness and self-control. Against such things there is no law. Those who belong to Christ Jesus have crucified the flesh with its passions and desires.
>
> —GALATIANS 5:19-24 (Emphasis mine)

As you can see, I have made bold some of the *acts* (fruit) *of the flesh* which relate to our study and included some definitions drawn from *Dictionary.com*[22]—hatred, discord (lack of harmony), fits of rage, dissensions (a strong disagreement or quarrel or a difference of opinion), and factions (cliques). Is the church immune to any of these? No. Are you? Probably not. Should these be part of our lives and of our testimonies? No. They are weeds that we need to pull up and remove from our lives. If left alone, they will choke out his Spirit in our lives and keep us from bearing fruit.

So how do we get rid of the *acts of the flesh*? Paul wrote, "Those who belong to Christ Jesus have crucified the flesh with its passions and desires" (Galatians 5:24). Did you notice that it says that those who belong to Christ have *crucified the flesh*...? Remember that the Cross is where love and forgiveness intersect. God loves us and we are supposed to love others. God forgave us and we are supposed to forgive others. That is how we crucify the flesh. Where there is love and forgiveness, *hatred, discord, fits of rage, dissensions* and *factions* can't survive!

Did you notice the strong warning that Paul included at the end of verse 21? "I warn you, as I did before, that those who live like this will not inherit the kingdom of God" (Galatians 5:21). Did you catch that? So, we have a choice: either we crucify the flesh with its passions and desires or we lose our inheritance in the kingdom of God. Are you going to let the weeds overtake your garden? I sure don't plan to!

God calls us to love and forgiveness. *Hatred, discord, fits of rage, dissensions* and *factions* should not be part of who we are. It will be painful to break these habits in our lives and uproot these weeds. But if we do, the fruit of the Spirit will begin to grow in our lives instead— *love, joy, peace, forbearance, kindness, goodness, faithfulness, gentleness, and self-control.*

> **If we do what Jesus commands us, he says that our reward will be great.**

So, what happens if you decide that crucifying your flesh is not your style? It's too painful and embarrassing to confess your mistakes to others and ask for forgiveness. Being on a cross can make you feel mighty exposed... Well, what's the alternative? Jesus said, "Every tree that does not bear good fruit is cut down and thrown into the fire" (Matthew 7:19). He didn't mince words or beat around the bush.

Our choices today have eternal consequences.

It's obvious that we need to *bear good fruit*, but how do we do it? Remember that the Bible is our instruction manual. It always offers the how-to for anything that God is requiring of us. Let's take a look at some of Jesus' last words to his disciples on the night before he was crucified:

> "I am the true vine, and my Father is the gardener. He cuts off every branch in me that bears no fruit, while every branch that does bear fruit, he prunes so that it will be even more fruitful. You are already clean because of the word I have spoken to you. Remain in me, as I also remain in you. No branch can bear fruit by itself; it must remain in the vine. Neither can you bear fruit unless you remain in me.
>
> "I am the vine; you are the branches. If you remain in me and I in you, you will bear much fruit; apart from me you can do nothing. If you do not remain in me, you are like a branch that is thrown away and withers; such branches are picked up, thrown into the fire and burned. If you remain in me and my words remain in you, ask whatever you wish, and it will be done for you. This is to my Father's glory, that you bear much fruit, showing yourselves to be my disciples."
>
> —JOHN 15:1-8

When we receive salvation, we are grafted into Jesus. Grafting is a process of removing a branch from one fruit tree or grapevine and attaching it to another in order to improve the fruit in some way. When we are grafted into Jesus, he becomes our root and the source of our life—as long as we remain in him. He said,

"Remain in me, as I also remain in you. No branch can bear fruit by itself; it must remain in the vine. Neither can you bear fruit unless you remain in me" (John 15:4). He didn't say "visit me." He said "remain in me." We need to do more than just visit Jesus on Sunday mornings, or when we're sick, or when life isn't going the way we planned. We need to stay connected to Jesus all the time. That is how we will bear fruit. If we don't remain in him, we will wither and die. Those aren't my words, they're his. "If you do not remain in me, you are like a branch that is thrown away and withers; such branches are picked up, thrown into the fire and burned" (John 15:6).

Remember that we learned at the beginning of our study that if something is really important, Jesus not only gives the commandment and repeats it, but he also tells us what the consequences are of not obeying. If we don't remain in Jesus, he says that we will wither and die and be "...picked up, thrown into the fire and burned" (John 15:6b). I don't know about you, but that seems pretty clear and direct to me. Would you rather bear much fruit or be burned up? The choice is yours.

Remain in Jesus. That is his commandment to us and his heart for us. The rewards are well worth it. Jesus said, "If you remain in me and my words remain in you, ask whatever you wish, and it will be done for you. This is to my Father's glory, that you bear much fruit, showing yourselves to be my disciples" (John 15:7-8). When we remain in Jesus, he will answer our heart's cry. He said, "ask whatever you wish, and it will be done for you" (John 15:7).

Later in the same chapter Jesus said, "You did not choose me, but I chose you and appointed you so that you might go and bear fruit—fruit that will last—and so that whatever you ask in my name the Father will give you" (John 15:16). Wow! Jesus said in this passage that he "chose us" and "appointed us to bear fruit." Can you feel his heart toward you? And yes, he said it again; in addition to bearing fruit, God will give us whatever we ask in Jesus' name as we remain in his love and obey his commandments (John 15:10). Jesus could make this promise to us because he knows that if we are found in him our requests will line up with his perfect will. We won't be asking for anything outside of what he already has planned for us. The price that we have to pay to remain connected to Jesus is nothing compared to the rewards that we will reap.

Plant intentionally into your life those things that you wish to harvest. Forgiveness is a must. Then, tend your garden by watering it with God's Word and removing any weeds that try to creep in and crowd out his life in you. Finally, if you want to bear fruit, remain in Jesus' love and make sure his words remain in you. Doing so will open up a whole new level of relationship with God where he promises to give you whatever you ask in his name. But don't forget that not remaining in him will lead to withering, dying and being burned up. The choice is yours each day. Plant into your life only those things that you wish to harvest. Choose forgiveness and choose life!

> **Plant into your life only those things that you wish to harvest.**

Forgiveness Story

Seeds of Bitterness

I was so excited! I could hardly wait for my friend Jacinda and her husband Esteban to show up. I had stayed up until 2:00 a.m. the night before, cleaning and putting final touches on the condo we were renting to them. It was hard to believe how fast the last two weeks had flown past. When my husband, Ricardo, and I found out that the Romeros needed a place to live, we had the condo we were fixing up almost completely redone. We still needed to install the new kitchen cabinets and counters and do some painting, etc., to finish things up by the time they needed to move in. Trying to finish everything up in time, with our already busy schedules, had been a challenge. It had thrown us into overdrive, but we were really excited to be renting to people we knew.

They were driving in. I couldn't wait to show Jacinda the granite countertops and nice cabinets that Ricardo had installed for them. We had agreed to rent the place partially furnished, and I had ransacked my own home to provide some homey touches to make them feel welcome when they moved in. I hoped Jacinda would like the chocolate that I had bought for the candy dish on the table and the other snacks I had brought over for them to munch on while they settled in. The whole place sparkled. I couldn't wait to see their reaction when they saw how nice everything was and how hard we had worked to make them feel welcome. I felt good inside. I had *done my best as unto the Lord*[23] and was *doing unto others as I would have them do unto me*,[24] like the Bible said.

The doorbell rang. They were here! Ricardo answered the door and Jacinda and Esteban walked in. Jacinda's reaction was not what I expected. She said hi quickly, and then started to walk around inspecting everything. There was no "Wow!" or "Thank you!" or "How cute!" like I had hoped—and to be honest, expected. Instead she started pointing out the pieces of furniture that she did not want and asking that we remove them. Before we left to get the truck to haul off the extra furniture, Jacinda did tell me that I didn't have to work so hard getting the place ready. But that was it. I was crushed! What a letdown! I had ignored my own house, my kids, and my other friends in an attempt to really honor the Romeros. What had it gotten me? "I don't need that recliner, and you can take the kids' bunk beds, too. Those curtains don't match my bedspread." All I knew was that things obviously weren't good enough for her. Despite all of my hard work, I had failed. Again.

Ricardo drove me home afterwards and I cried. I felt dead inside. Nothing mattered. Obviously, I didn't matter either. I could never seem to measure up to other people's standards. My mind started to run over situations in the past where I had tried unsuccessfully to please people. Whether it was my perfectionist mother, my sister Lola, my boss at work... The list was endless. The more I thought, the more dejected and rejected I felt. All I was lacking was a disco ball to get my pity party going full swing.

Then God brought to mind a prayer I had prayed a few weeks

back. *God, please remove any seeds of bitterness that I may be harboring. Help me to forgive quickly and not allow bitterness to take root in my life.* The music cut off and the lights came back on. My pity party was over.

It had all started with a video I had seen on YouTube. It had really shaken me up. This guy asked God to make heaven and hell real to him and said that if he did, he would share what he experienced with others. The condensed version is that he had a vision where he found himself before God's judgment seat. What really stood out to me was what he said about unforgiveness. He said that there were bad seeds in his heart and that God told him that they were from unforgiveness—even from situations and people he thought he had forgiven. When he protested, God told him that if he had truly forgiven the people, he wouldn't feel upset with them every time he spoke to them or thought about them. It was obvious that God was expecting more than just a perfunctory, outward forgiveness. He wanted a forgiveness that came from the heart.

There was a lot more to the video, but basically God told the man that he would forgive him the way he had forgiven others. If he forgave a lot, God would forgive him a lot. If he forgave a little, God would forgive him a little. That concept had really sobered me up. So, I had prayed. Now God was answering my prayer. Ouch! I realized that I had done all of that work over the last several weeks to please the Romeros—not to please God. I had done it to receive personal affirmation that I was *good enough*. The Romeros were not my problem at the moment. I could clearly see that unforgiveness in my past had taken root. God was letting the root of bitterness in me send up leaves and a stem so that I could recognize it, deal with it and pull it out. All of the times when I had worked hard to let people know they were special to me had really been my attempt to earn love and acceptance. God began to show me that only he can fill that void in my heart.

I had to let God shine a light on all the dark corners where bitterness had taken root because I hadn't received the acknowledgement that I thought I deserved. I had to truly forgive each one of the people from my past that came to mind and repent for doing things for people for the wrong reasons. Of course this was a process that took several months. (Needless to say, bitterness still pops out a branch from time to time even now and has to be dealt with).

During the time that God was dealing with me, it didn't take much for me to feel resentment towards Jacinda—even though I was in the process of trying to make things right with God and to forgive her. When my husband and kids told me that she had said that I had done a great job, I was upset that she hadn't told me herself. The thank-you note she wrote sparked another round of forgiveness. Eventually things began to get easier, and I began to recognize bitterness when it tried to sprout. Pulling up and removing some of its roots was really helping.

Then came the really hard part. Several months after they moved in, God told me that I had to go to my friend Jacinda and confess to her what I had been going through. I could never have done that if God hadn't been working in my life. Even then it was really hard. I went over to their place and asked Jacinda if I could talk to her for a few minutes. I told her that Satan had been trying to divide us because she hadn't responded the way I had wanted her to when she first moved in. I had to speak the truth to her even though it hurt and was embarrassing. We forgave each other. She forgave me for being distant and somewhat cold towards her since she had moved in. I forgave her for being so focused on her own needs that she hadn't seen mine.

The Bible says that the truth will set you free. I'm here to tell you that I was not the only person that was set free that day. Because of my obedience to do what God told me to do, not only was my relationship with Jacinda restored, but God in turn prompted her to go and make things right with several people that she had been holding grudges against. I wouldn't be surprised if the positive impact from that seed of forgiveness didn't keep multiplying out from there.

When we plant seeds of bitterness, that is what we will harvest. We forget that we will always reap more than we sow. By God's grace, Jacinda and I planted forgiveness and harvested its fruit instead of the fruit of bitterness.

When I stand before God's judgment seat, I don't want there to be any seeds of bitterness in me. I want to hear God say, "Well done, good and faithful servant!" (Matthew 25:23). I know I still have a ways to go, but at least I'm headed in the right direction again. And my friend Jacinda is walking beside me.

Seeds of Bitterness

After reading **Seeds of Bitterness,** answer the following questions thoughtfully:

1. Have you ever overreacted to a situation before? Did you realize you were overreacting, or did someone else have to tell you?

2. What do you think the difference is between *a seed of bitterness* and just plain *unforgiveness?*

3. Can you identify a seed of bitterness that is taking root in your life at the moment? What caused it?

4. In James 5:16 we read, "...confess your sins to each other and pray for each other so that you may be healed. The prayer of a righteous person is powerful and effective." Why does God want us to confess our sins to one another sometimes, instead of just forgiving each other privately in our hearts?

5. Can you think of a time when your obedience has borne positive fruit in other people's lives?

What does the Bible have to say?

Let's see what scripture has to say about bitterness and how we should deal with it when it takes root in our lives.

Hebrews 12:14-15
Make every effort to live in peace with everyone and to be holy; without holiness no one will see the Lord. See to it that no one falls short of the grace of God and that no bitter root grows up to cause trouble and defile many.

1. Many times the Bible talks about fruit. Why do you think bitterness is referred to as a root? How is a root different from fruit?

2. Do you recognize any roots of bitterness in your life? List three ways you can begin to dig up these roots and remove them from your life.

Ephesians 4:31-32
Get rid of all bitterness, rage and anger, brawling and slander, along with every form of malice. Be kind and compassionate to one another, forgiving each other, just as in Christ God forgave you.

1. What is bitterness associated with in verse 31? Do you think that any of those other actions are the fruit or result of allowing a root of bitterness in your life?

2. Who are you imitating when you are kind and compassionate and forgive others? Can bitterness survive in this environment?

Acts 8:22-23
Repent of this wickedness and pray to the Lord in the hope that he may forgive you for having such a thought in your heart. For I see that you are full of bitterness and captive to sin.

1. Are just your actions important to God, or do your thoughts matter too? Why?

2. When you are full of bitterness, what are you a prisoner of or captive to?

PRAYER

Father God, I come before you today and ask that you would give me a true spirit of repentance. Lord, search my heart today and shine your light on any unforgiveness or roots of bitterness that I have harbored and allowed to take root and grow in my life. I pray that you would help me to dig deep and recognize what has opened the door for this bitterness to infiltrate my heart. Strengthen me by your Holy Spirit to recognize and deal with the underlying causes. Help me not to fall short in showing your grace and love to those around me. Help me to forgive others the way you have forgiven me—fully, completely, and without bearing a grudge or keeping a record of the wrong. Please heal the broken places in my life that make me susceptible to harboring bitterness. I pray that your love would wash over me and overflow to the lives of those around me. In Jesus' name, Amen.

Memory Verse:

Choose one of the previous passages that you would like to learn and make a part of your spiritual arsenal. Copy it down using your preferred Bible translation and memorize it.

_____

_____

_____

_____

In the blink of an eye everything can change, so forgive often and love with all your heart. You may never know when you may not have that chance again.

—Zig Ziglar

APPENDIX

F	Focus on God's grace and mercy and how much he has forgiven you.
O	Offer the offense up to God and release it to him.
R	Repent for any judgmental feelings or feelings of anger toward the person who offended you.
G	Give thanks to God that he will bring good out of what happened.
I	Invest in praying for the person who offended or hurt you.
V	View the other person through God's eyes. He loves them!
E	Erase the repetitive voice of the enemy from your thoughts by blessing the one who hurt you every time the person or situation comes to mind.

Who forgives all your sins...

—PSALM 103:3

Get rid of all bitterness, rage and anger, brawling and slander, along with every form of malice. Be kind and compassionate to one another, forgiving each other, just as in Christ God forgave you.

—EPHESIANS 4:31-32

Do not judge, or you too will be judged. For in the same way you judge others, you will be judged, and with the measure you use, it will be measured to you.

—MATTHEW 7:1-2

And we know that in all things God works for the good of those who love him, who have been called according to his purpose.

—ROMANS 8:28

...pray for those who persecute you

—MATTHEW 5:44

But God demonstrates his own love for us in this: While we were still sinners, Christ died for us.

—ROMANS 5:8

We demolish arguments and every pretension that sets itself up against the knowledge of God, and we take captive every thought to make it obedient to Christ.

—2 CORINTHIANS 10:5

Bless those who persecute you; bless and do not curse.

—ROMANS 12:14

ND
Forgiveness Worksheet

After reading the **F O R G I V E** acrostic, think of one or two people that you know you need to forgive.

Write down their first names or initials:

_____   _____

PRAY:

For the next two weeks, take time every day to go through the steps listed in the **F O R G I V E** acrostic, and pray for the person/people on your list. Initial beside each day after you have done so. It does not matter what day of the week you start on.

Week One:

Monday:_____

Tuesday:_____

Wednesday:_____

Thursday:_____

Friday: _____

Saturday:_____

Sunday:_____

Week Two:

Monday:_____

Tuesday:_____

Wednesday:_____

Thursday:_____

Friday: _____

Saturday:_____

Sunday:_____

Now that you are done, when that person comes to mind, how do you feel? Can you feel your attitude changing? If you feel peace when you think of the person now, the bulk of your forgiveness process may be over. However, sometimes the smallest things can retrigger feelings of animosity or unforgiveness. If that happens, don't worry. Just repeat the forgiveness process for as long as it takes to reset your mind and thought patterns.

Continue to choose names to focus on forgiving and repeat the process until your heart is clear.

Memory Verses:

Memorizing the verses listed will help you to forgive more readily and will keep bitterness from taking root in your heart. Copy them down below using your preferred Bible translation, and check them off as you can recite them from memory.

____ Psalm 103:3

_____

_____

_____ Ephesians 4:31-32

_____

_____

_____

_____

____ Matthew 7:1-3

_____
_____
_____
_____
_____

____ Romans 8:28

_____
_____
_____
_____

____ Matthew 5:44

_____
_____
_____

APPENDIX

____ Romans 5:8

_____
_____
_____
_____

____ 2 Corinthians 10:5

_____
_____
_____
_____

____ Romans 12:14

_____
_____
_____

Should you stay in an abusive relationship?

Please read the following disclaimer before starting this part of our study on forgiveness.

Disclaimer: Are you in an abusive relationship? If so, the first thing you should do is enlist professional help. I am not a licensed counselor, psychologist or psychiatrist. The purpose of this section is to help those of you who believe that as a Christian you have to stay with your abuser and forgive them or you're not obeying God. That is not true! Hopefully this study will help you to better understand what the Bible says on the topic of forgiveness under circumstances of abuse.

Based on your own experiences or those of people you know, answer the following questions thoughtfully:

1. Does forgiving the other person always solve the problems in a relationship?

2. Does forgiving mean that you must agree to continued abuse? Why or why not?

3. Have you ever found yourself in a relationship where it was time to leave but you were having a hard time letting go? Did you let go? What helped you make that decision? Are you glad you did?

4. What type of boundaries does God want us to have in our lives?

5. Does God command us to forgive *everything*? Why? How is forgiving an important component of the healing process?

What does the Bible have to say?

The story of David and Saul is one of the best representations of a love/hate abusive relationship in the Bible. David chose to flee and set up boundaries. But he also forgave Saul and did not hold a grudge against him or cause him harm.

Read 1 Samuel chapters 18-24, 26, and 2 Samuel 1 to get a good picture of David and Saul's relationship. When you're finished, answer the following questions:

1. When Saul pretended to be nice to David, even offering his daughter to him as a wife, what were his true intentions? (1 Samuel 18:17)

2. Was Saul trustworthy? Did he keep his word? (1 Samuel 19:6-9)

3. Did David plan revenge against Saul or forgive him? (1 Samuel 24 and 26)

4. Did David come back to live in the royal court when Saul apologized and promised not to try to harm David? In your opinion why not? (1 Samuel 26: 21-25)

5. What was David's reaction when he heard of Saul's death? (2 Samuel 1)

6. How did he still view Saul despite their past history? (2 Samuel 1:14)

7. What are three (or more) important lessons that we can learn from this relationship?

8. How did David "reap what he sowed" later on when he became king? (2 Samuel 22)

PRAYER

Father God, thank you for your love for me. Thank you that you promise wisdom to any who will ask. Today, you and you alone understand the place that I find myself in. Please give me supernatural wisdom and understanding in my current situation. Help me to hear your voice clearly and follow whatever directions you give me. Please confirm to me what you would have me do, so that I won't second guess myself or any decisions that I need to make right now. Help me to establish appropriate boundaries as needed. Thank you that I am in the palm of your hand. Help me to rest securely in your care for me. I also ask that you would help me to forgive those who have sought to do me harm. You are their judge. I am not. I pray that they may come to know your saving grace as I have. Please forgive them Lord, as you have forgiven me. In Jesus' name I pray, Amen.

Memory Verse Options:

Proverbs 4:23 (NLT)
Guard your heart above all else, for it determines the course of your life.

Proverbs 22:3 (NLT)
A prudent person foresees danger and takes precautions. The simpleton goes blindly on and suffers the consequences.

Proverbs 26:23-26 (NLT)
Smooth words may hide a wicked heart, just as pretty glaze covers a clay pot. People may cover their hatred with pleasant words, but they're deceiving you. They pretend to be kind, but don't believe them. Their hearts are full of many evils. While their hatred may be concealed by trickery, their wrongdoing will be exposed in public.

You have just read several proverbs that were written by Solomon, David's son. He was considered one of the wisest men that ever lived. Choose one that you would like to learn and make a part of your spiritual arsenal. Copy it down using your preferred Bible translation and memorize it.

_____

_____

_____

_____

_____

_____

Endnotes

1. Matthew 5:44 KJV.
2. Ibid.
3. Ibid.
4. Hymn by John H. Samms, 1887.
5. Strong's Lexicon at https://biblehub.com/parallel/matthew/18-24.htm (Accessed May, 25, 2020.)
6. Ibid.
7. James Strong, "Matthew 18:24," Strong's Lexicon. Bible Hub: https://biblehub.com/parallel/matthew/18-24.htm (May 25, 2020).
8. https://biblehub.com/parallel/matthew/18-28.htm (Accessed May 25, 2020) and Strong's Concordance pg. 1601
9. Adapted from Luke 6:31.
10. David B. Guralink, ed., "Bitter," Webster's New World Dictionary, 2nd College Ed. (New York: Simon & Schuster, 1984), 145; "Resentment," 1209; "Cynical," 353.
11. Guralink, "Anger," 52; "Rage," 1172.
12. Guralink, "Brawl," 172; "Slander," 1337.
13. Guralink, "Malice," 857.
14. Exodus 34:6; Numbers 14:18; Nehemiah 9:17; Psalm 86:15; Psalm 103:8; Psalm 145; Joel 2:13; Jonah 4:2 (ESV).
15. James 2:13b.
16. Masoretic text.
17. Paul is quoting from Isaiah 45:23.
18. To put it into proper context, you may need to read Genesis 50 first.
19. Clarification mine.

20 "As," Merriam-Webster. Merriam-Webster.com: https://www.merriam-webster.com/dictionary/as (May 24,2020); "For," Merriam-Webster. Merriam-Webster.com: https://www.merriam-webster.com/dictionary/for (May 24, 2020).

21 Adam Clarke, "Matthew 6," Commentary on the Bible. Bible Hub: https://biblehub.com/commentaries/clarke/matthew/6.htm (May 24, 2020).

22 "Discord," Merriam-Webster. Merriam-Webster.com: https://www.merriam-webster.com/dictionary/discord (May 24, 2020); "Dissensions," Merriam-Webster. Merriam-Webster.com: https://www.merriam-webster.com/dictionary/dissensions (May 24, 2020); "Factions," Merriam-Webster. Merriam-Webster.com: https://www.merriam-webster.com/dictionary/factions (May 24, 2020).

23 Colossians 3:23.

24 Matthew 7:12.

Bible Translations

Scripture quotations marked ESV are taken from the ESV® Bible (The Holy Bible, English Standard Version®). ESV® Text Edition: 2016. Copyright © 2001 by Crossway, a publishing ministry of Good News Publishers. The ESV® text has been reproduced in cooperation with and by permission of Good News Publishers. Unauthorized reproduction of this publication is prohibited. All rights reserved.

Scripture quotations marked KJV are taken from the King James Version of the Bible.

Scripture quotations marked NKJV are taken from the New King James Version®. Copyright © 1982 by Thomas Nelson. Used by permission. All rights reserved.

Scripture quotations marked NLT are taken from the Holy Bible, New Living Translation, copyright © 1996, 2004, 2015 by Tyndale House Foundation. Used by permission of Tyndale House Publishers, Inc., Carol Stream, Illinois 60188. All rights reserved.

We would love to hear how this book has helped you along your forgiveness journey.

Please send your comments to
490lovestudy@gmail.com.

www.ingramcontent.com/pod-product-compliance
Lightning Source LLC
Chambersburg PA
CBHW051343040426
42453CB00007B/381